MODERN NOVELISTS

General Editor: Norman Page

MODERN NOVELISTS

Published titles

Forthcoming titles

MODERN NOVELISTS
BARBARA PYM

Michael Cotsell

St. Martin's Press   New York

All rights reserved. For information, write:
Scholarly and Reference Division,
St. Martin's Press, Inc., 175 Fifth Avenue, New York, NY 10010

First published in the United States of America in 1989

Printed in Hong Kong

ISBN 0–312–02054–6

Library of Congress Cataloging-in-Publication Data
Cotsell, Michael.
Barbara Pym.
(Modern novelists)
Bibliography: p.
Includes index.
1. Pym, Barbara – Criticism and interpretation.
I. Title. II. Series.
PR6066.Y58Z64 1989   823'.914   88–4443
ISBN 0–312–02054–6

Contents

Acknowledgments

I am most grateful to Mrs Hilary Walton and Mrs Hazel Holt for permission to consult and quote from the Pym collection in the Bodleian Library. In addition I am grateful to Mrs Holt for her kind and helpful responses to my letters and enquiries. My thanks also go to the staff of the Bodleian Library, Oxford, for making the material available and for their assistance.

I am grateful to Macmillan Publishers for permission to quote from *The Sweet Dove Died, Quartet in Autumn, A Few Green Leaves, An Unsuitable Attachment*, and *A Very Private Eye: An Autobiography in Diaries and Letters*, ed. Hazel Holt and Hilary Pym. Also to Jonathan Cape Limited for permission to quote from *Some Tame Gazelle, Excellent Women, Jane and Prudence, Less than Angels, A Glass of Blessings* and *No Fond Return of Love*.

I gratefully acknowledge Faber and Faber Limited for permission to quote from 'High Windows' from the book *High Windows* by Philip Larkin; Faber and Faber and Mr Andrew Motion for permission to quote from Philip Larkin's letters to Barbara Pym; the Estate of Elizabeth Taylor and William Heinemann Ltd and A. M. Heath & Company Limited for permission to quote from letters of Elizabeth Taylor to Barbara Pym; and Lord Jonathan Cecil for permission to quote from letters of Lord David Cecil to Barbara Pym.

I am deeply indebted to Professor Edward Nickerson of the English Department of the University of Delaware who read the entire typescript and suggested many improvements of style and presentation. Such inelegancies as remain are, of course, my own. I am also grateful to my research assistants, Donald Brown and Patience Phillips, who collected the reviews of Pym discussed below, and to Patience Phillips for preparing the bibliography. The University of Delaware provided a grant for the preparation of the typescript, which was typed by Suzanne Potts.

Finally I would like to thank Professor Harry Bloom, of the State University of New York at Oneonta, and Mrs Dorothy Bloom who introduced me to Pym's work.

General Editor's Preface

The death of the novel has often been announced, and part of the secret of its obstinate vitality must be its capacity for growth, adaptation, self-renewal and even self-transformation: like some vigorous organism in a speeded-up Darwinian ecosystem, it adapts itself quickly to a changing world. War and revolution, economic crisis and social change, radically new ideologies such as Marxism and Freudianism, have made this century unprecedented in human history in the speed and extent of change, but the novel has shown an extraordinary capacity to find new forms and techniques and to accommodate new ideas and conceptions of human nature and human experience, and even to take up new positions on the nature of fiction itself.

In the generations immediately preceding and following 1914, the novel underwent a radical redefinition of its nature and possibilities. The present series of monographs is devoted to the novelists who created the modern novel and to those who, in their turn, either continued and extended, or reacted against and rejected, the traditions established during that period of intense exploration and experiment. It includes a number of those who lived and wrote in the nineteenth century but whose innovative contribution to the art of fiction makes it impossible to ignore them in any account of the origins of the modern novel; it also includes the so-called 'modernists' and those who in the mid- and late twentieth century have emerged as outstanding practitioners of this genre. The scope is, inevitably, international; not only, in the migratory and exile-haunted world of our century, do writers refuse to heed national frontiers – 'English' literature lays claim to Conrad the Pole, Henry James the American, and Joyce the Irishman – but geniuses such as Flaubert, Dostoevsky and Kafka have had an influence on the fiction of many nations.

Each volume in the series is intended to provide an introduction to the fiction of the writer concerned, both for those approaching him or her for the first time and for those who are already familiar with some parts of the achievement in question and now wish to place it in the context of the total *œuvre*. Although essential information relating to the writer's life and times is given, usually in an opening chapter, the approach is primarily critical and the emphasis is not upon 'background' or generalisations but upon close examination of important texts. Where an author is notably prolific, major texts have been selected for detailed attention but an attempt has also been made to convey, more summarily, a sense of the nature and quality of the author's work as a whole. Those who want to read further will find suggestions in the select bibliography included in each volume. Many novelists are, of course, not only novelists but also poets, essayists, biographers, dramatists, travel writers and so forth; many have practised shorter forms of fiction; and many have written letters or kept diaries that constitute a significant part of their literary output. A brief study cannot hope to deal with all these in detail, but where the shorter fiction and the non-fictional writings, public and private, have an important relationship to the novels, some space has been devoted to them.

NORMAN PAGE

For Maeve

Introduction

Barbara Pym was born on 2 June 1913, in Oswestry, a small town in Shropshire. She attended Huyton College, Liverpool, and in 1931 entered St Hilda's College, Oxford, graduating three years later with a BA, with second class honours, in English. Between 1934 and 1939 she lived mostly at home. During this period she drafted *Some Tame Gazelle*, which failed to find a publisher, and a number of unpublished novels, the manuscripts of which are in the Bodleian Library. In 1940, Pym left home to work in the Postal and Telegraph Censorship in Bristol and in 1943 joined the Wrens (Women's Royal Naval Service). Between 1944 and 1945 she was stationed in Italy. In 1945 she returned to London and in 1946 took a post as a research assistant with the International African Institute, where she continued to work until 1974. In 1945 she began to revise *Some Tame Gazelle*, which was published by Jonathan Cape in 1950. Cape then published *Excellent Women* (1952), *Jane and Prudence* (1953), *Less than Angels* (1955), *A Glass of Blessings* (1958) and *No Fond Return of Love* (1961). In 1963, *An Unsuitable Attachment*, the seventh novel she submitted to Jonathan Cape, was unexpectedly rejected. Nor could other publishers be interested in *An Unsuitable Attachment* or its successors *The Sweet Dove Died* and *Quartet in Autumn*, the latter written after Pym had undergone an operation for cancer in 1971. A change in her literary fortunes came with the publication in 1977 of a special edition of *The Times Literary Supplement* in which both Lord David Cecil and Philip Larkin named her the most underrated writer of the previous seventy-five years. *Quartet in Autumn* was published in 1977 and was a Booker Prize finalist. *The Sweet Dove Died* was published in 1978, and Pym's last novel, *A Few Green Leaves*, appeared in 1980. Pym died on 11

1

January 1980. A revised version of *An Unsuitable Attachment* was
published in 1982 with a foreword by Philip Larkin. Since then,
her literary executor, Hazel Holt, has published two other
novels, *Crampton Hodnet* (1985) and *An Academic Question* (1986).
With Hilary Pym, Barbara's sister, Hazel holt has also published
*A Very Private Eye: The Diaries, Letters and Notebooks of Barbara
Pym* (1984). Pym's reputation is now well established on both
sides of the Atlantic and she has recently been the subject of a
number of critical books and articles. Barbara Pym is now
generally recognised as one of the leading British novelists in
the period since the Second World War.

Her works have the essential virtues of the traditional novel:
they create convincing and interesting worlds peopled by living
and engaging characters. One of the early admirers of her work,
Lord David Cecil, wrote to her in 1953, 'You have so much
sense of reality and sense of comedy, and the people in your
books are living and credible and likeable. I find that rare in
modern fiction. Thank you very much' (Bodleian Library, MS
Pym 148). John Bayley, in a letter to Philip Larkin, punned to
define this quality, calling it her 'novelty' (MS Pym 152).
Readers have delighted in her eye for the little ludicrous
moments in the texture of all our lives. Her contemporary the
novelist Elizabeth Taylor wrote to her of *Jane and Prudence*,

> It is all one's own life, but made interesting, colourful & even
> exciting. Something to remember as one works about the
> house, something to keep one company. I shall never see a
> thermometer-case, foie gras in Fortnum's, or even the window-
> cleaner's ladder appearing at the lavatory windows without
> thinking of you.   (MS Pym 162)

It would be difficult to say as much of a D. H. Lawrence or a
Robbe-Grillet.

Barbara Pym writes in the tradition of English social comedy
that runs from Jane Austen to the early works of E. M. Forster.
She was, however, influenced at different stages in her career by
writers who, from differing perspectives, call the world of that
English social comedy into question: Aldous Huxley, Elizabeth
Bowen, Ivy Compton-Burnett, and others, as well as by
European writers such as Chekhov and Proust. The Second
World War deepened her sense of history, and the social

developments of post-war Britain impressed upon her the passing of that world. Nor could she fail to be aware of modern codes of interpretation (the Freudian and others), and her work at the African Institute encouraged her to perceive social behaviour with some of the anthropologist's detachment.

The characteristics of her fictional world were established early, however. Her evocation of jumble sales, church fêtes, tea-drinkings, the drab offices of civil servants, wet holidays in dull English hotels, a little longing for the sun of Italy or Greece, is a selection of English experience recognisable to millions of readers as somehow essentially and absurdly English. Its high potential for comedy derives from the tendency of its inhabitants not quite to connect with the grand event or the grand passion, but to proceed with a baffled, tireless, good-natured commitment to sustaining the genteel. In Pym, the inhabitants are almost uniformly single persons of middle-age, men and women attached to careers no more functional or demanding than the clerical (in this view) or the academic, and freed from the intensities and destinies of generation. Parents are rare in her novels, children rarer; relations are characteristically at a remove – uncles or aunts, nephews or grown children. Her presentation has nothing in common with that of such a writer as Beckett – she is far too warm and amusing in her appreciation of the texture of ordinary lives – but nevertheless pointlessness and futility are everywhere felt in her novels, serving to give a significance at once comic and poignant to little moments of feeling and details of behaviour. It is characteristic of her vision that life can be compared, by one of her most lively heroines, to an elderly female relative:

> Life had been going on for Catherine too, as she knew that it would. She thought of it as an old friend, or perhaps a tireless elderly relative, pushing, knocking, clinging, but never leaving her alone, having the power to grant her moments of happiness but being very stingy with them just now.
>
> (*Less than Angels*, ch. 13)

Comedy is of the essence of Pym's art, a comedy that is inseparable in her work from a certain order of female point of view, open to registering the apparently insignificant details of behaviour in which we are most revealed. Inevitably the male is particularly detectable in these respects:

> 'Such a pity Hilary can't be with us this evening,' said Rodney rather formally to James Cash.
> 'Is she ill? I didn't quite gather,' said Sybil bluntly.
> 'Well, not really. She has just had a child,' said James in a rather surprised tone. . . .
> 'One never *quite* knows what wine to drink with gooseberries,' said Rodney, turning to James Cash rather apologetically. . . .
> 'Perhaps they are more a woman's fruit,' said Sybil, 'like rhubarb. Women are prepared to take trouble with sour and difficult things, whereas men would hardly think it worthwhile.'
> The men were silent for a moment, as if pondering how they might defend themselves or whether that, too, was hardly worth while. Rodney's next remark showed that they had evidently considered it not to be.
>
> (*A Glass of Blessings*, ch. 1)

Philip Larkin wrote in *The Times Literary Supplement* that 'Miss Pym's novels may look like "women's books", but no man can read them and ever be the same again' (1977). Whether that is the whole truth is doubtful. There is something flattering, as well as something unnerving, in the degree of attention the novels pay to men. Men are finally indulged in Pym's fiction, for, as Catherine Oliphant perceives in *Less than Angels*, behind the mask cowers 'the small boy, uncertain of himself' (ch. 21). Men seem to like this view. Pym has appealed to readers of both sexes, but she has been more popular among the generation of male critics represented by Lord David Cecil, A. L. Rowse and Philip Larkin than among feminist readers. Perhaps this is partly because the novels are unabashedly romantic (Pym was for some time a member of the Romantic Novelists' Association). As Belinda, the middle-aged heroine of *Some Tame Gazelle*, reflects, 'Besides, it was really more suitable to lavish one's affection on somebody of a riper age, as it was obviously natural that one should lavish it on somebody' (ch. 17). And, if the novels have an unerring eye for male insensitivity and egoism, they offer the male reader the alternative role as the true appreciator of the undervalued woman, the man with the eye for the violet by the mossy stone. It is somehow in keeping with Pym's fictional world that her novels should have been, first, insensitively rejected by the ambitious men at Cape, who preferred to publish what she called novels about 'men and Americans', and then rescued through the loyalty of the traditionalists, Cecil and Larkin.

Pym's account of female experience, though often amusing, is by no means simply comfortable. Her fiction, it has been widely observed, has as a central focus the shock of disappointment and rejection. Her heroines have repeatedly to cope with feelings of neglect, desolation and loneliness. The theme of disappointment and the perception of underlying futility suggest the potential crisis with which her characters and their author have to deal. Where Pym fundamentally differs from the braggadocio of some male modernist writers (hard-riding existentialists, profuse Joyceans, insistent nihilists) is in her refusal to identify with meaninglessness – which is also a refusal to separate art from our human need to make meaning in our lives. Meaning must be sustained amongst us by good humour, a delight in the absurd, recurrent small gestures, taking an interest, loving anyway. Life delivers disappointments but if those disappointments are accepted – the virtue is humility – small joys and satisfactions still await us. Art is a way of sustaining a humorous and hopeful engagement with life. One of the attractions of Pym's novels is that we sense in them the author's own repeated commitment to hopefulness, the repeated act of imagining possibility. If we sometimes detect in her what she explores in some of her characters, a refusal at some level of life and relationship, we can also admire the candour of her exploration and her delight in the range of experience she does allow herself.

Creation, in the sense suggested above, is a theme in her novels: the creation of an interest in life. Pym was as much a reader of poetry as of novels, and her novels and characters often arrive at quiet moments of poetic beauty and intensity. Noting that the entry was made one week after the beginning of the Second World War, Pym copied into her Commonplace Book (MS Pym 83) the poem 'The Cherry-Blossom Wand' by Anna Wickham. The first and last stanzas read:

I will pluck from my tree a cherry-blossom wand,
And carry it in my merciless hand
So I will drive you, so bewitch your eyes,
With a beautiful thing that shall never grow wise.

If this seems too intense, too Yeatsian, for Pym's novels, nevertheless, it suggests her commitment to an art of romance and delight. On the other side can be placed an entry from a diary written late in life:

> When the priest prays for the sick of the parish the names sound like those of well-known novelists (mostly female of course) —
>
> Elizabeth Jane Howard
> Iris Murdoch
> or
> Emily Bronte [*sic*]
> Jane Austen
> Maria Edgeworth   (MS Pym 86/1)

The tradition of great English women writers becomes a parish of ageing women preparing for death. Pym's novels move between, even blend, the perceptions embodied in these two passages, the living impulse to love and art, the awareness of how we grow older, stouter, plainer, and (single or married) how we die like elderly ladies or gentlemen of the parish.

This study attempts to describe the main features of Pym's art. The novels are discussed in the order in which they were written; each discussion, though it connects to other parts, is complete in itself. I have provided some biographical and historical context, but the reader who wishes to know more about Pym's life is referred to *A Very Private Eye* and Hazel Holt's forthcoming biography. As Lord David Cecil recognised, Pym's novels are readily enjoyable by the ordinary reader, as perhaps many contemporary novels are not. I have tried to bring out their essential pleasures and concerns, and hence I have had much to say about the characters, their loves and their lives.

I have also drawn on some of the modes of criticism which are important and influential today, though none of them is formally presented and argued. It has seemed important to show that Pym's novels can answer to the kinds of critical inquiries we characteristically make of contemporary literature. This cannot pretend to be a feminist work, but any study of Pym must keep in mind that its subject is a woman author, exploring one phase of women's experience. I have not drawn explicitly on Marxist or other historicist criticism, but I have asked questions about the relation of Pym's work to the historical developments of her time. I have also discussed Pym's work in relation to contemporary structuralist and post-structuralist accounts of language with the intention of suggesting that a fiction such as hers cannot be conceived as 'traditionalist' where that word implies 'naïve' or 'unreflecting'. With this in mind I have also traced some of Pym's relations to modernist art.

Pym began to write in her teens, and the writer's interest in the world and in writing is a theme in a number of her works. Her commitment to her art is demonstrated not just by the published novels, but by the unpublished novels and short stories, and the large number of notebooks and diaries now in the Bodleian Library. The lively interest the diaries and notebooks demonstrate is the source of what Philip Larkin called 'the richness of detail and variety of mood and setting' (MS Pym 151–2) in the novels. A small group of entries from the notebook for 1948–9 (MS Pym 40) must serve to exemplify Pym's qualities of observation:

Dulwich – 1st Sunday in September
Times Ed Sup in the lavatory – a pair of dirty white gym shoes on the mahogany edge of the bath.
Feeding the cats of a friend who has gone away – almost sacramental procession of herrings, cooked in [*illegible word*] dish covered with a plate and wrapped in newspaper – eyes dropping out
Breaking up of a scholar (as E. P.) – little carping criticisms, no constructive work.
Archaeology – a dig is not 'amusing'

Pym, it might be said, was in love with experience, as some of her characters are in love with difficult men: the rewards of a continuing lively interest exceed the frustrations and

disappointments. Whether in the midst of a heart-breaking love
affair or hospitalised for a critical illness, she records her
experiences with a wonderful perception and quick reflection.
This capacity owes something to an undogmatic religious faith,
much more to an open humorous spirit.

There has not been space in this study to draw extensively on
the diaries and notebooks. I have, however, given some account
of the unpublished novels (Chapter 2) and have briefly sketched
the stages of composition for the published novels. Generally,
the first ideas for the novels, deriving from things Pym has
seen, or involvements in her own life, are recorded in her little
literary notebooks (MSS Pym 39–82). In one, for instance, we
can find the first note for *A Glass of Blessings*:

WHAT IS MY NEXT
NOVEL TO BE?

It can begin with the shrilling of the telephone bell in Freddie
Hood's church – and end with the flame springing up – the
new fire sprung up on Easter Saturday, in the dark church.
Hope and a blaze of golden forsythia round the font.
   But what about the middle?   (MS Pym 46, fo. 15r)

When a novelist can think in images in this way, we resist the
distinction between poetry and prose. As is shown below
(Chapter 4) the middle was not immediately or easily established,
but from this note we can see that the essential feeling of the
novel is captured at once. Once she had the initial idea or ideas
for a novel, Pym established a notebook or notebooks in which
she recorded the succession of further ideas, shaped and altered
her conception of characters and events, pondered titles and
sketched scenes. There was then a draft – usually much
corrected – and then at least a second draft of the novel before
the final typescript. To study the processes of composition is to
enjoy a delightful intimacy that confirms the stature of Pym's
art.

1

Oswestry and Oxford: Early Writings, Literary Influences, and *Some Tame Gazelle*

Barbara Pym employs a limited range of settings in her novels, based on places she knew in her own life, each of which has a certain value for her. Those places are Oswestry, her childhood home; Oxford; London; and localities abroad with which she was familiar: Germany and, later, Italy. Oxford and London appear as themselves; Oswestry is the model for all the villages and country towns in the fiction; and Germany and Italy, places of rather unreal romance, appear sometimes as themselves, sometimes as Hungary or Finland. Together they make up her imaginative world, the geography of her feelings.

Barbara Pym was born in Oswestry and spent her childhood there. After her studies at Oxford were completed she returned to live at home until the advent of the war. Oswestry is a small town in Shropshire. Such towns were, for the class to which she belonged, affected only mildly by the great changes that swept across English society in the nineteenth century, so that they are often now regarded (and not only by those who inhabit them) as the real England. Pym's father was a solicitor and a respectable member of the Church of England. Both her parents were of good family, though her mother's father had risen in trade. She enjoyed a comfortable and untroubled childhood, the family home 'a substantial, square red-brick Edwardian house with a large garden on the outskirts of town' (*A Very Private Eye*, p. 2); the family kept two maids, who slept upstairs, and of whom one acted as nanny, and there was a pony for pulling the governess cart. It is a world well described for us by Hilary Pym, Barbara's younger sister, in *A Very Private Eye* (pp. 1–7). she also tells us that, because of a knee injury, Barbara's father, Frederick Pym, was not called up for service during the First World War. It is not difficult to sense a continuity between the world of Pym's childhood and Edwardian and Victorian England.

The repeated appearance in the fiction of scenes drawn from life at Oswestry is a sign that for Barbara Pym there was no great quarrel with her past or upbringing. Family, in which her mother and sister figure larger than her father, appears in her fiction as a kind of security and continuity, with all its little domestic doings and minor irritations. The relationship between sisters is particularly strong. A recurrent comedy is derived from a sibling awareness of burgeoning sexual interest: the attention to curates is but one instance ('Having curates to supper was a long-established tradition', Hilary Pym tells us). This is not to say that there is not at times a feeling of constriction and irritation in Pym's repeated evocations of family life, particularly in the unpublished novels written after her years at Oxford and before the war, when life seemed to offer very little in the way of alternatives. Even in her earliest works there is some degree of restiveness: Pym was desirous of experiencing life and from an early age ambitious to be a writer. Yet Oswestry and family were always there in her imagination, as something bright and comfy and humorous. It is, of course, a sign of this attachment that she lived for much of her life with her sister Hilary; Hilary was briefly married, and Barbara had a number of sexual relationships, but in the end neither made a home away from family. Oswestry and family represent warmth and security in Pym's fiction, and the development of her fictional world might, therefore, be figured forth as the gradual dispersal of its sense of community into a larger urbanised scene, as though the small town had grown, friends became more distant and familiar places smaller or harder to find; as though new and unknown people had moved in, office blocks and council flats sprung up; the church, though still there, somehow out of place in its new surroundings.

It is, however, notable that the figure of the father is absent from Pym's evocations of the domestic scene. Without a full biography, there is little to base speculation on, but it is likely that this absence is a key to understanding a fictional world (and a life) which is characterised by the elusiveness of the male (an elusiveness which is given emphasis in the treatment in two of the novels, *A Glass of Blessings* and *The Sweet Dove Died*, of a woman's misplaced interest in a homosexual male). In this context it is worth looking ahead to draw attention to a group of events at the end of the war. In September 1945 Pym's mother died and the following year her father remarried. Also in 1945 Pym opened her notebook for the revised version of *Some Tame Gazelle*. In 1946 Hilary Pym separated from her husband and the two sisters began to live together. A full biography may allow us to understand the connections between these events.

Pym's happy comic inventiveness derives from the good humour of her family life, and by her teens she had already begun to think of herself as a writer. At her school, Huyton, she led the Literary Society, and by the age of seventeen she had completed her first novel, 'Young Men in Fancy Dress', which survives in a fair copy manuscript (MS Pym 1). It is dedicated to one 'H. D. M. G.', 'Who kindly informed me that I had the makings of a style of my own'. A style of her own had become important to her, and, though 'Young Men in Fancy Dress' is in many ways a typical piece of juvenilia, it does show Pym consciously considering the problem of style and in so doing laying the ground of much of her subsequent fiction.

'Young Men in Fancy Dress' is the story of a young would-be writer, Denis Feverel, named, Pym indicates, after a character in Huxley's novel *Crome Yellow*. Denis, the self-conscious son of a nouveau-riche sausage-manufacturer, wishes to be an original and a writer. The novel begins,

'He took nobody by surprise, there was nobody to take.' Denis laid down his pen to consider the words that he had just written. He said them aloud and meditated upon their subtle humour with pride. Then a sudden and horrible thought occurred to him. The words seemed familiar. Where could he possibly have heard them before? – no relative or friend of his was capable of saying anything like that.

He got up and paced about the room in a state of alarm. While thus occupied he noticed a book lying upon the mantel piece. The title seemed to rise and hit him between the eyes –

he felt stunned and in a moment the terrible truth flashed
upon him. The phrase he had written was one that he had
read in that book – one which had struck him at the time as
being a delightful example of humour. Yes – he remembered
it all now. With a short cynical laugh – which was altogether
unnatural – he sat down again and crossed out the offending
words, with a firm hand.   (fos 1–2)

Denis's phrase is from Huxley's *Crome Yellow* (1921), which
seems to him 'about as perfect a novel as could be' for it is 'Not
actually about anything – of course not – the best novels never
are – but full of witty and intelligent conversation.' (fo. 3).
Rather than be himself, Denis seeks to be a character in such a
world: 'Denis longed above all things to be different from other
people. He succeeded but did not seem to realise the fact' (fo.
4). Events launch Denis into a literary and social career
amongst Bohemian young men in London, but after a time he
becomes disillusioned with the people he had once sought: 'You
all behave as if you were at a fancy-dress ball – that's what I
think' (fos 119–20). He does not return to the glad arms of his
upbringing 'He knew that it was wicked of him but he couldn't
help admitting that his father and mother annoyed him more
than almost anyone else in the world' – fo. 23) but he has
begun to find himself by the novel's inconclusive ending.

'Young Men in Fancy Dress' offers a wealthy, carefree young
people's world, untroubled by constraints or duties – all literary
discussion and posing and a certain gauzy romanticism, girls
turning their faces up to be kissed under street lamps, and so
on. More importantly, the novel shows Pym establishing her
own style and fictional world by a process of parody of a
fictional influence and a self-deprecating humour, which is also
the affirmation of a choice and a self – as Denis is different from
other people when he ceases trying to be so. As the narrative
progresses, a more appropriate Denis begins to emerge, one
who is, in a rather priggish phrase, 'always ready to listen to
his elders and his betters', and who has – an important element
of Pym's fiction – 'the power to feel excited about the smallest
things, for which he always felt rather thankful' (fo. 123).
Rather than the cult of style, an ethical and lively commitment
to the ordinary world produces the possibility of an emergent
artist.

It is particularly interesting that 'Young Men in Fancy Dress' is developed out of a response to a relatively modernist text, Huxley's *Crome Yellow*. The relation of parody is, of course, complex. Pym's novel follows Huxley's work (and his *Those Barren Leaves* [1925]) even as it departs from it. Like *Crome Yellow*, as it is described by Denis, Pym's novels are apparently 'not actually about anything', or not about very much, and are full of conversation, which is amusing if not always witty. But, in being about nothing, Pym's novels also affirm something, the little gestures and commitments, the feelings and doings of the ordinary day, so that her work is at once an imitation and a rejection of the sophisticated, intellectual Huxley world. As will be repeatedly shown in this study, Barbara Pym's fiction is often developed out of a shifting relation, partly of acceptance, partly of rejection, to modernist texts; this relation, while it obviously does not make her a modernist herself, demonstrates that the development of her fiction cannot be seen as flowing in an unbroken stream from the Victorian and Edwardian novel, unpolluted by an alien modernism. Like Philip Larkin, whose early work assimilates and then rejects Yeats, Pym can usefully be described as a post-modernist.

Three stories in a manuscript notebook of this period, 'Poetry and Prose 1931', also introduce pretentiously artistic young men encountering normality, and another, 'Death of a Young Man', tells of how a poetic novelist murders a prosaic young man so that he can write about the experience. It is interesting that Pym's fictional world is early defined by its imaginative employment of such young men and then the rejection of their pretensions for more ordinary values. This is partly a woman writer defining her realm in reaction to the clever literary young men to whom she was naturally drawn. It is possible to go further, though, and say that such a young man, literary, pretentious, knowing, and modern, is her imaginative animus, in the dual sense of a figure towards whom she feels a certain animosity, but one who is also the figure of her imaginative aspiration, the animus that is the male counterpart of the anima in Jung's account of the psyche. It would be in keeping with the cultural relations between the sexes in Pym's era that, whilst in male fiction the anima often occurs in an idealised form (a form that is also a subtle reduction), in her fiction the animus must be presented within a comic resistance.

The young men in fancy dress attract her and annoy her, even hurt her, but she is also, as writer, a young woman in fancy dress. Pym expresses some of her own ambitions through such figures but is also engaged in a rivalry with brilliant young men that is not wholly concealed by humour or romantic devotion. It is easy to see that certain personal disappointments were to contribute to Pym's fiction, less obvious that her ambition to write was always strong, that she was competitive, and that her writing gave her a power over experience, and a freedom from it, even as she was experiencing. At any rate, it is striking that just as her later setting-up of home with Hilary is anticipated in *Some Tame Gazelle*, so her relationship with Henry Harvey (see below, Chapter 2) is in some measure anticipated in her early fiction. Life here imitates art not just because the art is already deeply structured by life, but because the demands of the art are already imposing patterns and choices.

That 'Young Men in Fancy Dress' is a response to the fiction of Aldous Huxley shows that Pym was already reacting strongly to literary influences. The novelists with whom she is most frequently compared are Jane Austen, Trollope, the Mrs Gaskell of *Cranford* and *Wives and Daughters*, and E. M. Forster. Austen figures in her diaries and correspondence, and there are repeated allusions to her work in Pym's novels (the critical discussion of Austen's influence is described in Chapter 7). It may be said that, rather than being influences in any very direct way, those earlier major novelists who were staple reading for anyone of literary interests from Pym's background provided a basic ground for her fiction, an agreed preliminary characterisation of the England in which she grew up.

Her father admired Kipling, and perhaps both sides of his fiction, the humorous expansive side and the private melancholy side, touched her. She was also an enthusiast for a form to which the English are much drawn, the detective novel (her spy novel, 'So Very Secret', is really a detective novel). All her life, Hilary Pym and Hazel Holt tell us, Pym was addicted to exuberantly playing detective, following and finding out: she practised this sleuthing on Henry Harvey at Oxford, for instance, and it is introduced as a conscious device for making the world around one interesting in *No Fond Return of Love*. As a teenager, Pym read Edgar Wallace, and the less well-known Frank Darrell; later she enjoyed Dorothy L. Sayers' *Gaudy Night* which combined the detective powers of Lord Peter Wimsey with an Oxford women's college setting. Detective novels of the genteel kind, from Sayers to Agatha Christie to P. D. James (whose work in some respects resembles Pym's), are a feature of her time. Their attraction, one might suppose, is the combination of humorous gentility and quiet ingenuity exercised in close proximity to, but ultimate distance from (the gulf between the detective and the criminal), passion, sensation and vice. The corpse turns up in the living-room of the nicest people; something runs under the surface, with which one is implicated, but from which the regularly produced 'solution' finally absolves one. A detective novel is a flirtation secured by a final frigidity: something that Pym at times accuses herself of.

From the basis of Oswestry and the normative tradition, Pym, as we have seen, began early to engage with modernism, first with the novels of Huxley, later with Ivy Compton-Burnett, Henry Green, and others. Her reaction is never simply one of rejection, but it always involves some resistance. She was often put off by the subject matter of modernism, finding Ibsen's *Ghosts* horrible and terrifying, and von Stromberg's film *The Blue Angel* horrid and depressing. So also she disliked the novels of Ivy Compton-Burnett at first, finding *More Women than Men* unreal, though Compton-Burnett proved more difficult to resist. This debate with modernism entered into her relations with Henry Harvey.

From her female contemporaries it is difficult to detect much influence, with the exception of the Anglo-Irish novelist Elizabeth Bowen. Bowen's pathetic and sadly comic evocations of the declining lives of the Anglo-Irish gentry had a certain appropriateness for Pym as she moved away from the securities of her Oswestry and pre-war world; nevertheless, there is great difference between her style and Bowen's mannered lyricism. Pym later admired the novels of Elizabeth Taylor, with whom she corresponded, but Taylor's style lacks Pym's humour and vivacity. In the 1960s, when her hold on the development of her fiction became unsure, she seems to have looked to Margaret Drabble and perhaps Muriel Spark for guidance, but the results were not happy.

Judging from the letters and diaries of her Oxford years, the novel did not loom as large in her reading as poetry did. The Oxford English degree at this time was primarily philological.

The serious student (and Pym seems to have felt she was never quite that) sought to develop a command of the details of the tradition and the mysteries of Old English and medieval textual studies. The aggressive moralising of Leavis at Cambridge had not made itself felt, though modernism was exciting the interested student: cubist painting; exhibitions of Man Ray in London; Joyce and Eliot. Eliot's rereading of the poetic tradition away from Victorian poetry and towards the more austere virtues of the seventeenth century is partly what accounts for Barbara Pym's apologetic tone about her taste for the Victorians: 'What a bad sign it is to get the *Oxford Book of Victorian Verse* out of the library' (*A Very Private Eye*, p. 40). Oxford English was certainly then untainted by what we now call literary theory, and if one was not going to become an academic or a librarian (as Pym's male friends did) then to read English was to read a great deal of English poetry, major and minor, with some doubt that one was perhaps only collecting useless adornments, but with a real feeling of personally discovering the beautiful and delightful.

If sentimental minor Victorian poetry was an indulgence, she was also drawn to the Romantics, particularly Keats, and to seventeenth- and eighteenth-century poetry: on the latter, Cassandra, the heroine of her third novel, reflects, 'What funny things the eighteenth-century poets chose to describe in verse. . . . In spite of the austerity of their poetry they were very homely, and she loved them for it' (MS Pym 5, fo. 27). Pym liked a poetry that said things finely about romantic situations and sentiments that we all experience – 'sentiments to which every bosom returns an echo' is a line about which she jokes in *Some Tame Gazelle* – and she is more struck by the quotable line or passage than by the structure or overall scheme of poetic works.

This taste for 'our greater English poets', as she often humorously calls them, is at least as important for an understanding of her fiction as any account of the influence of novelists. It is a familiar fact that her novels usually draw their titles from poems and that they frequently allude to poetry. In fact, the majority of her successful novels have a poetic text or texts as a kind of focus of the feeling about the world they proffer; each is formed around a preliminary poetic characterisation of the field, and this characterisation is extended through allusion and imagery into the texture of the novel. Pym is not a poetic novelist in the manner of Virginia Woolf or Elizabeth Bowen, but her essential feeling for the world has the richness, wonder and concentrated emotion of the poetic.

Pym's 1934 Notebook or Commonplace Book (MS Pym 83) demonstrates both her love of the poetic tradition and her painful romantic involvement with Henry Harvey. Entitled 'My Love in Literature', it is actually a hurt and aggressive collection of quotations, from Pope, Randolph, Young, Milton, Thomson and others, in which Harvey each time appears as the smooth-tongued seducer and hypocrite (the passage from Milton, for instance, is the description of Belial in *Paradise Lost*, book II; from Pope's *The Rape of the Lock*, that beginning 'There *Affectation* with a sickly mien'). Since the relationship with Harvey is so important for her literary development, it must be discussed here.

From the beginning, it appears, Pym embarked on a rather heady and over-excited romantic career at Oxford. There is much that is amusing and delightful in her account of her involvements and self-dramatisations, but it does also seem that in her exuberance and desire to carry off an impression she was more sexually free than she could emotionally cope with and thus exposed herself to hurt and to humiliation.

The great excitement came from meeting Henry Harvey, an undergraduate some years older than she. In Pym's diaries he was 'Lorenzo' (after the unfortunate character to whom Young addresses his *Night Thoughts*), she 'Sandra'. The haughty, slightly affected style of Harvey and his friends – if that was what it was – excited an attempt to impress him and then a love the depth of which surprised and deeply pained her. It is tempting to see Harvey as a priggish, arrogant young man, the man who did not realise, who gave up the love of a Barbara Pym for a merely conventional relationship. Certainly some of the novels encourage us to make such a reading, and perhaps there is some truth in such a view. Nevertheless, Pym must have been, to use a colloquial phrase, a handful, bringing to the relationship an outpouring of romantic enthusiasm but also a cleverness at once doting and very remarking. Whosoever the fault, when the couple had sexual relations Harvey immediately began to retreat. He covered his confusion and discomfort by at times adopting, or being driven to, a cruel taunting or indifference. It is clear that Pym felt sexually humiliated.

Perhaps the fear of sexuality that is a theme in some of the later novels largely derives from this early experience.

The details of this relationship are conveyed in the extracts from Pym's diaries and letters in *A Very Private Eye*. A more appropriate emphasis for this study is on the 'literary debate' between the couple which can be discerned in the letters that passed between them after Harvey had left Oxford to take up a lectureship in Finland. Early in 1936 Pym recorded in her diary that she had received 'a long letter from Henry, but as it was written in Latin, German, French, Swedish, Finnish and the English of James Joyce, I could not well understand it' (*A Very Private Eye*, p. 78). This use of learning and the obscurities of modernism to avoid direct emotional confrontation clearly pained Pym. In a letter of her own of May, she picked up a phrase of Harvey's, 'we have never been real to each other', and commented on an affected style, apparently current in their circle, that clearly bears relation to modernist literary theories of the persona, the mask, the 'flat' self, and the self-as-fiction. As in her early novels, she is on the side of the ordinary:

> It is an amusing game, and I don't see why it should affect one's real self unless one wants it to. I know that as far as I am concerned, although I've learned to treat things in his way, the other side of me is still there to be brought out when necessary. I have no wish that it should be annihilated altogether because I know I couldn't find any happiness unless I were a real person as well as a 'flat' one.
>
> (*A Very Private Eye*, p. 80)

The term 'flat', of course, derives from E. M. Forster's distinction in his *Aspects of the Novel* (1927) between 'flat' and 'rounded' characters: Pym, the traditionalist, like Forster, prefers the 'rounded' character and life. But Henry held all the cards: when he visited England that year he played records of Joyce to her, and by December 1937 he had married a Finnish woman. Her letters to the couple, which pour out her hurt, attempt to cover it in a display of cleverness, a pastiche of Joyce, the films and Ivy Compton-Burnett, completely at odds with the style of the novel ('Beatrice Wyatt': see below, Chapter 2) she announces she is working on:

And this novel it is oh-so sober and dull, and there are no parties of young people getting *beschwipst,* and there are no Finns or Swedes or Germans or Hungars and the *Magyar bor* is not flowing freely at all, and there is no farm on the *puszta* ... no, there is none of this. Well, there can be really nothing, you say. And you will be right *die ganze Welt dreht sich um Liebe* you will be saying in a fury, *sentimentvolle Stimme* as you see darling Henry and more darling Elsie and how happy they are. And you will be coming back to England, and you will be meeting this so dull spinster which is like the old brown horse walking with a slow majestic dignity, and you will be saying Well-fer-goodness-sake, Miss Pym, like they say in the films. But this spinster, this Barbara Mary Crampton Pym, she will be smiling to herself – ha-ha she will be saying inside. (*A Very Private Eye,* p. 96)

The young man in fancy dress had temporarily imposed a modernist style on Pym, to which her novel is a retort, a reassertion of herself and her terms. Nevertheless the relation to modernism here is complex. Modernism represents a false, external, clever masculine influence which she seeks to repudiate, but it is also the language of an immediate disorder and pain in herself. In excluding modernism, Pym is thus not simply excluding an alien influence, but excluding or concealing a painful awareness of herself. By choosing to exclude modernism, she confines her fictional world to English social comedy. The best of her subsequent novels find ways to allow in elements of the 'modernist' perspective, but usually in the form of a distancing anthropological knowledge. This element of repression in Pym's fiction is typical of post-Second World War British writing. It is interesting that in this letter she goes on to mention the 'so nice poems of Mr Betjeman': the discovery of a voice that made a light, though sometimes pained, poetry of suburban trivia and Anglicanism must have confirmed her in her choice.

The first version of *Some Tame Gazelle* was written between 1934 and 1935. Pym was not successful in finding a publisher, though she received some encouragement, and the novel was abandoned until, at the end of the war, in 1945, she began to make notes for an extensive revision. The revised novel was accepted by Cape and published in 1950.

It is thus important to recognise that *Some Tame Gazelle*, as we have it now, is not the product of the 1930s, but emerged from a writer who had by then drafted half-a-dozen other manuscript novels and whose life had moved well on from the experiences which initially stimulated the work. The first version arose directly from her Oxford years and the affair with Harvey. The heroine Belinda is based on Pym herself ('Sandra' was her name for herself in her diaries); Harriet on her sister Hilary; and the majority of the other characters on members of her Oxford circle – Harvey is Archdeacon Hoccleve, who has married not Belinda but Agatha, who is based not on Harvey's Finnish wife but on Barbara's Oxford rival for Harvey's attentions. The first version thus preceded the final extinction of Pym's hopes of Harvey. It was partly conceived as something on which she and her Oxford friends might look back together – as a *jeu d'esprit*, perhaps even her achievement to place alongside the academic achievements that had made her feel uncomfortable and even inferior. Through the novel she was talking to them.

What is striking about even the first version of *Some Tame Gazelle* is that in it Pym immediately established her characteristic fictional world. Hilary Pym has remarked that the novel's scenario of two single, middle-aged sisters living together precedes the event in real life. Pym's novelistic world and her major characters are more diverse than is sometimes remembered, but, all the same, the fictional ground is laid here. First, and primarily, there is a single woman heroine disappointed in love, loving rather than loved. As in most of her novels, it is the point of view of this heroine which is adopted for the tale, and her neglect is a source of both pathos and humour:

> 'He – er – said you did a lot of work in the parish,' replied the curate primly.
> 'Oh . . . .' Belinda could not help feeling disappointed. It made her sound almost unpleasant. (ch. 1)

Again, as in the majority of the remaining novels, the church provides a focus, though what really links the characters together is human love: 'Was there anybody in the church without some romantic thought?' (ch. 22). Pym registers the comic and touching flow of desire through this dull, respectable church world.

This establishing move can perhaps be seen as Pym bringing her Oxford life back to Oswestry. We have seen that at Oswestry were family, security, sibling warmth, a place for the affections which Pym had exposed to hurt at Oxford. The feeling of home (the two sisters: Barbara did not live with Hilary at Oxford) and of home doings in the novel strongly suggests this. Again, the church was an important part of Oswestry life. The novel was written after Pym graduated, and while she was living much of the time at home. Her feelings of disappointment in love doubtless led her to perceive her relatives and neighbours in a new way.

A deepening of the sense of acceptance distinguishes the two versions of the novel. The earlier version has many scenes of conversation and plot relations that are later excised, and the overall tone is more facetious (there is a continuing debt to Huxley). The later version has greater sentiment and focuses more on Belinda's feelings, and her fidelity to the past; it is striking that, in the notebook in which she plotted the revisions, Pym indicated that she had recently been reading Proust's fiction and Chekhov's play *The Cherry Orchard*. The move towards a greater focus on Belinda's feelings is indicated by the plot shift recorded in the 1945 note 'Can the Bishop propose to Belinda?!' and then the rough plan for chapter 21: 'Belinda ill. Bishop proposes to Harriet, and is rejected. Triumph and vindication. Bishop proposes to Belinda' (MS Pym 3, fo. 2v). By giving Belinda the dubious privilege of the proposal from Bishop Grote, Pym moves her towards the centre of joy she discovers is still present in her life. Furthermore, in the earlier version Agatha does not have any feelings for the Bishop – so that Belinda cannot feel her small triumph over her – nor so much a part of the wedding of the curate. Equally significant in this respect is a group of 1945 notes made under the heading 'Domestic details'. They show an increasing attention to Belinda's domestic world though once again a key experience is at first given to Harriet: 'Harriet is making macaroni – it must be kneaded for *half an hour*. Quote that bit out of the cookery book' (MS Pym 3, fo. 4v). This is the germ of one of the most attractive of Belinda's moments in the final version. What Pym achieves in these changes is the introduction of a feeling that gives a deeper poetry to the texture of literary allusions in the work.

All the major characters of *Some Tame Gazelle* have had a literary education. Harriet's study of the classics provides her well-corseted plumpness with some suitably roguish moments: at one point she and her current curate are discovered reading the Roman erotic poet Catullus. This is a private joke, for Hilary Pym took classics at Oxford. Harriet's admirer, the somewhat unlikely Count Ricardo, sighs over the classics and Dante. Agatha Hoccleve is a medievalist, and hence serious (an illusion characteristic among medievalists); her niece, Olivia Berridge, who will marry Harriet's curate, is even more serious, a don who is doing work on *The Owl and the Nightingale*, and Agatha likes to feel that she regrets the lost opportunity herself.

The novel's greatest literary enthusiast is the Archdeacon, whose splendid comic wilfulness is reminiscent of Trollope's Archdeacon Grantly in *Barchester Towers*. The Archdeacon – Henry Hoccleve – is an enthusiast for the melancholy of seventeenth- and eighteenth-century poems, notably for Young's *Night Thoughts*. His taste for the 'graveyard school' leads him to enjoy striking melancholy poses in the churchyard. His taste for Milton, and especially for reading Milton to the admiring Belinda, nicely recalls the blind poet's demands on his unwilling daughters. Hoccleve is also 'blind' to other's feelings. Pym discerns that the grandiloquence of expression of certain poets and the pretension of scholarly learning belong very much more to the male than to the female. Even Belinda's favourite Victorian poets do not escape this perception:

> *The trivial round, the common task* – did it furnish *quite* all we needed to ask? Had Keble *really* understood? Sometimes one almost doubted it. Belinda imagined him writing the lines in a Gothic study, panelled in pitch-pine and well dusted that morning by an efficient servant. Not at all the same thing as standing at the sink with aching back and hands plunged into the washing-up water.   (ch. 20)

'Had Keble *really* understood?' nicely parodies the earnest tutorial question. Great literature does not quite fit the world Belinda lives in:

Yes, one of those with a quotation from Shakespeare or a
Great Thought for every day. I always think it's nice to have
one in some convenient place so that you can read it at the
beginning of the day. And yet the thoughts they choose are
often so depressing, aren't they, as if Great Thinkers were
never cheerful.   (ch. 18)

At the novel's comic centre is the day on which the
Archdeacon chooses most inappropriately to deliver two long
sermons on Judgement Day, not because he feels its imminence,
but as the occasion for many of his favourite quotations. The
sermons conclude with T. S. Eliot:

> 'Oh, it was beautiful,' gushed Connie Aspinall, 'I did so
> enjoy it.'
> The Archdeacon looked pleased. 'I had feared it might be
> rather too obscure,' he said. 'Eliot is not an easy poet.'
> Belinda gasped. Eliot! And for the evening congregation!
> But it must have been magnificent to hear him reading
> Eliot.   (ch. 11)

And the Archdeacon goes on to consider giving a course of
sermons on Dante. Eliot has been mentioned earlier, when
Belinda discovers, to her horror, a caterpillar in her seamstress's
cauliflower cheese:

> And then, in a flash, she realized what it was. It was almost
> a relief to know, to see it there, the long, greyish caterpillar.
> Dead now, of course, but unmistakable. It needed a modern
> poet to put this into words. Eliot, perhaps.   (ch. 4)

It should be clear that Eliot is not being taken wholly seriously.
The Archdeacon is, in fact, a modernist: he has picked up the
taste for Eliot and for the poetic tradition that Eliot had marked
out. By comparison, Belinda's taste is shamefully unregenerate:
her criteria are sentimental and populist.

Some Tame Gazelle thus carries on Pym's debate with Harvey
about modernism. What Pym sets against the Archdeacon's
taste is the reality of feminine experience and feeling, the little
daily commitments and pleasures on which the male ego
unconsciously depends. Belinda's favourite quotations lack

pretension but they have a homely application which the Archdeacon's do not. She seeks in literature the expression of

> '*Sentiments to which every bosom returns an echo,*' said the Archdeacon. 'Yes, one appreciates that, and yet, why shouldn't Eliot express those sentiments?'
>
> 'Do the bosoms of people nowadays return any echo?' said Mr Mold. 'One wonders really.'   (ch. 11)

It is a telling and more than comic touch that the well-known line suggests the middle-aged faithful women present as audience to this exchange of male cleverness. Nicholas Parnell, the librarian, has summed up the male conceit with the quotation from Johnson (which suffices for him): '*Love is only one of many passions and it has no great influence on the sum of life*' (ch. 11).

Some Tame Gazelle is not a simple rejection of modernism, however. Rather, it is a humorous and perceptive reworking of assumptions and practice. Pym accepts what might be said to be the dramatic premise of *The Waste Land*, that we possess only scraps of the cultural tradition: 'Perhaps it was hardly suitable, really, and she was a little ashamed of having quoted it, but these little remembered scraps of culture had a way of coming out unexpectedly' (ch. 5). But in her work they do not gather together to the big solemn voice of Culture; they exist in the ordinary life as ornaments, pleasures, focuses of interest, expressions of our moods. There is always an incongruity between their portent and our lives: an incongruity, it might be said, that Eliot could not finally accept. In this refusal to bring together all the voices, it might be said that Pym constitutes a post-modernist art, but what it accepts from modernism must also be recognised. Pym identifies her effect as *antiphonal*, a term from church music, but one that also suggests the compositional principles of works such as *The Waste Land*: 'So the sisters continued antiphonally, each busy with her own line of thought.' In Pym, the antiphony continues within the ordinary life: 'But at last they found themselves in agreement on the subject of Harriet's brown velvet dress' (ch. 4). Pym's comedy depends on this play between diverse, unmeeting private desires and the ordinary every day co-operations that life demands. This is the 'music' which, in her view, the male poet, undergraduate or cleric, harking after greater chords, cannot hear.

Not a great deal actually happens in *Some Tame Gazelle*; this is characteristic of Pym's novels. Belinda's favourite two quotations are as banal as could be: 'Hope springs eternal in the human breast' and 'God moves in mysterious ways'. Between them they suggest an ordinary openness to life that may not satisfy us as we hope, or expect, or anticipate, but nevertheless has its pleasures. Belinda has recurrent moments of quiet joy. The first 'movement' of the novel concerns the events at a church fête and the episode of the caterpillar. Belinda's joy comes from the release from her feelings of guilt about her poor, rather bitter seamstress and from her feelings of inferiority to Agatha Hoccleve:

> Belinda's eyes filled with tears and she experienced one of those sudden moments of joy that sometimes come to us in the middle of an ordinary day. Her heart like a singing bird, and all because Agatha didn't keep as good a table as she did and Miss Prior had forgiven her for the caterpillar, and the afternoon sun streaming in through the window over it all. 'You're doing that chair cover *beautifully*, Miss Prior,' she said warmly, 'and how well you've got on with Miss Harriet's dress.' (ch. 4)

Her joy takes the form of expression of kind trite words, just as the response of Miss Prior to her (which included the bonus of the information about Agatha's comparative meanness to her dressmaker) was produced by an obvious concern for her feelings. Pym's art brings us not to lonely universals but to necessary recurrent acts of goodness and warm-heartedness.

This early movement anticipates in miniature the movement of the whole. Belinda is reminded of her lost hopes by the absence of Agatha Hoccleve on holiday in Karlsbad, and the resulting little intimacies with the Archdeacon. In chapter 13 she has a brief opportunity to taste again the joys of her undergraduate days. But Agatha inevitably returns. Otherwise the two events of the novel are in the nature of non-events. A visiting librarian of slightly vulgar manners proposes to her sister, but is rejected. Then unexpectedly, a visiting Bishop, who has been staying at the Archdeacon's, proposes to Belinda and is in turn rejected. The proposal scene itself provides the opportunity for comedy at the expense of male egoism:

'When I was a younger man I held views about the celibacy of the clergy, young curates often do, you know,' he smiled indulgently, 'it is a kind of protection, if you see what I mean. But a man does need a helpmeet, you remember in *Paradise Lost* . . .

Belinda interrupted him with a startled exclamation. '*Paradise Lost!*' she echoed in horror. '*Milton* . . .' (ch. 20)

But again there is an unexpected bonus for Belinda, for she knows that Agatha has rather liked the Bishop herself:

It was not until they were in the hall that she realized that she had been offered and refused something that Agatha wanted, or that she may have wanted, for the hint she had given had been very slight. (Ibid.)

And then:

To think of Agatha as pathetic was something so new that Belinda had to sit down on a chair in the hall, quite overcome by the sensation. She began to find ways of making things better and more bearable. (Ibid.)

It is not just that Belinda has a triumph over Agatha, but that she feels that Agatha like herself is capable of pain (there is another bonus later when she somehow gathers that Agatha proposed to Henry). It is at this particular point, whilst kneeding dough for ravioli, that Belinda has her perception about Keble. And then the joy comes quite quietly, beautifully signalled by the established code of imagery of the preparation of food:

'Oh, Harriet, *look!*' Belinda held up the sheet of ravioli she had been rolling.

'But, Belinda, it's just like a piece of leather. I'm sure that can't be right,' protested Harriet.

'It is,' said Belinda joyfully, 'it's even finer than the finest chamois leather.' (Ibid.)

Belinda has discovered what she has been working at all along: the fine consistency of her life.

The novel ends with a marriage, an English Hymen Io, the marriage not of Belinda or her sister, but of Harriet's curate and the woman don, Olivia Berridge. Like the 'widowed' Tennyson in *In Memoriam*, which also ends with an epithalamion, Belinda will be true to her past love. Comedies end with marriages, but the characters we find most interesting and like ourselves are not necessarily the young hero and heroine at the altar. Nothing has happened and nothing will happen. With her head full of quotations, appropriate and ridiculous, Belinda realises that

> she too was happier than she had been for a long time.
>
> For now everything would be as it had been before those two disturbing characters Mr Mold and Bishop Grote appeared in the village. In the future Belinda would continue to find such consolation as she needed in our greater English poets, when she was not gardening or making vests for the poor in Pimlico. (ch. 22)

To which she adds, 'Dr Johnson had been right when he had said that all change is of itself an evil.' There is nobody in the church without a thought of romance, but Belinda has brought her romantic thoughts and churched them. In doing so, she chooses her life.

2

Towards War: *Crampton Hodnet* and the Unpublished Novels

After her studies at Oxford were completed, Barbara Pym slipped into a restless life divided between Oswestry and Oxford. Despite the unsatisfactory state of her relationship with Henry Harvey, and his departure to teach in Finland, she still had hopes of him. When, in 1937, Harvey married a Finnish woman, Elsie Godenhjelm, Pym was, Hazel Holt tells us, 'badly hurt' (*A Very Private Eye*, p. 13). To distract herself (it may be said), Barbara Pym had twice again visited Germany and there continued her light-hearted affair with Friedbert Gluck. Then in 1937, after Harvey's marriage, she began a 'very consciously Romantic' affair with an Oxford undergraduate six years younger than she (ibid., p. 15). But, with the Second World War, Barbara Pym's life at Oswestry and Oxford was brought to a close: she was caught up in the war effort, moved to London and then Bristol, and, in 1943, after another romantic complication, joined the Wrens. In July 1944 she was posted to Naples.

Though Pym's life drifted until the war took it up, her commitment to her writing was constant through the period until her departure for Italy. Between the completion of the first version of her first novel, *Some Tame Gazelle*, and the early notes (1945) for her next published novel, *Excellent Women*, she drafted the whole or part of seven novels, which, with the exception of *Crampton Hodnet*, have to date not been published. *Crampton Hodnet*, the most successful of these works, was published with an introduction by Hazel Holt in 1985. These novels are primarily set in Oswestry and Oxford, and bear close relation to

the events in their author's life. The earliest of them show Pym's
continuing preoccupation with Harvey and her disappointment
over his marriage. The novels then draw on her trips abroad and
with her affair with the Oxford undergraduate. The impact of the
war is registered in an unfinished war novel, 'Amanda Wraye',
and a spy novel, 'So Very Secret'. Between these two last she
wrote *Crampton Hodnet*, in which she achieved a successful artistic
distance from her Oxford world. None of her subsequent novels is
set there.

The first of the novels after *Some Tame Gazelle*, 'Civil to
Strangers' (MS Pym 5), was written in 1936. It is a light
humorous piece which derives from Pym's continuing optimism
about her relationship with Harvey. The heroine, Cassandra,
has been married for five years to the peevish minor novelist
Adam Marsh-Gibbon. Though a little disappointed with
married life, she is the perfect wife:

> At one time she used to pray in her prayers that she might be
> saved from doing anything that Adam might not like, or that
> would be unsuitable to the position she held in the town, but
> lately she had left it out of her petition. It was no longer
> necessary, she thought, and was sometimes a little sad that
> this should be so.   (fo. 19)

The tiresome Adam is nicely presented: he is a Wordsworthian,
writing novels about '"the beautiful and permanent forms of
nature"' so that 'some times she almost wished that Wordsworth
had never been born' (fo. 113). The writer-husband is
demanding: 'At this moment Adam came back into the room.
He had his "I am not inspired and you may try to amuse me
but you won't succeed" expression on his face' (fo. 223). The
story tells how their marriage is rejuvenated when Cassandra
apparently runs off to Budapest with a Hungarian; evidently
Pym's 1935 visit to Germany lies behind it.

'Civil to Strangers' is slight, though enjoyable, infused as it is
with a romantic optimism: 'O blessed marriage! thought
Cassandra' (fo. 308). It is the only one of Pym's novels that is
enthusiastic about children, and at its end we learn that
Cassandra is going to have a baby. The nicest comic effects
derive from the heroine's peculiar and excessive sensitivity to
the possible bearings of a commonplace remark. This is not just

feminine sensitivity, but a position at once inside and outside the socially acceptable. Trying to please a young girl, Cassandra praises her flower arrangement for the church:

> 'I thought it looked so cool, like an oasis,' she added, and then felt that this was a silly comparison, as it implied that the rest of the church was like a desert, and was thus uncomplimentary to the rector and the congregation.   (fo. 5)

Though self-accusing, the thought allows the mind to follow, even as it is embarrassed by, an emotion that is not quite in accord. The sense of surface and undercurrents in social discourse is, as we have seen, characteristic of Pym's narrative style. It also constitutes a large part of the charm of her heroines, their particular order of femininity: sophisticated but naïve; finely mannered, but without hard edge, since there is always an accompanying emotion; poised, as it were, between coolness and a blush; socially perfect but with an alluring hint of subversive feelings and thoughts which never quite constitute a threat.

The next novel, 'Beatrice Wyatt; or, The Lumber Room' (MS Pym 6/1–3) exists only in a rough draft which evidences many marks of artistic and emotional indecision, and, towards its conclusion, weariness and lack of conviction. It is separated from 'Civil to Strangers' by the great gulf of Harvey's marriage and is marked by melancholy and by a degree of bitterness and hostility to the Oswestry life to which Pym now seems to have felt confined. Pym scalds and scolds her own femininity in the presentation of the women around her. The harshly portrayed Mrs Wyatt lives with her two daughters, the religious and irritable Frances, and Beatrice, who is an Oxford don. A new curate, Stephen Bone, comes to the parish. In a much corrected and then entirely rewritten chapter, (ch. 6), Beatrice and Stephen are first shown coming together romantically, then the possibility of Stephen being engaged is introduced, and finally Stephen is revealed to be engaged. Stephen then marries his fiancée, a Pre-Raphaelite beauty, a 'strange inhuman arti-crafty looking figure in green' (fo. 102), who makes him a bad wife (the decline of their marriage owes something to the David and Dora scenes in *David Copperfield*). Beatrice herself pursues an affair, which she knows to be incongruous, with a young undergraduate, successively named in the manuscript as Lawrence Otway, Gerald Cleveland, and, finally, Hughie Otway. This relationship does not last (Hughie is drawn to the Pre-Raphaelite beauty), and in the last chapters 'Henry', Beatrice's old love, returns to her, his wife having conveniently died. 'The Lumber Room' clearly demonstrates Pym's inability to make anything of her emotional predicament at this time, and there are few even moderately effective scenes. The image of the lumber room, a room filled with the furniture of the old life, a place of memories, though not well-developed, is of interest since it appears in subsequent writings. Another point of interest is the number of allusions to the 'International Situation'.

The next novel (MS Pym 7), an untitled Finnish novel, also written in 1938, is even weaker. Gervase goes to Finland to lecture, where there is comedy of a predictable kind about the English 'colony' and his affairs with young and unconventional Finns. He is followed to Finland by Flora, his longstanding admirer, who, realising her passion for him is hopeless, generously aids the Swedish girl he does finally marry. Flora herself becomes involved with a genial and drunken Finn called Ooli: Pym has blended an imaginary Finland with her holidays in Germany. The evocation of Finland is understandably slight, though an attempt is made to make the long Finnish winter stand for the oppressive gloom that can enter into lives. Otherwise the work has little merit.

Were proof necessary, the existence if this series of unpublished works would show how important the disappointment over Henry Harvey was for Pym's fiction. The Harvey affair established in her writing the centrality of the theme of disappointment and its overcoming through fidelity to memory (in 'Beatrice Wyatt' we read that Hughie is too young 'to have a nice lumber room mind like Beatrice' – MS 6/1–3, fo. 172). It would be mistaken, however, to see the affair as an explanation of all the subsequent fiction, for what the novels of this period conclusively prove is that, when the emotion over Harvey was dominant, Pym was not a successful novelist. These are the most autobiographical of Pym's novels, more so even than *Some Tame Gazelle*, in which the Oxford circle is recast in a middle-aged world; and the heroines of these works are simply projections of Pym herself, their experiences workings-out in fantasy of her own situation. In the published novels there is some continuity of heroine type, and of structure of emotions, but the heroines are by no means Pym herself, nor are their situations simply her own. Her achievement as a novelist would not be what it is if each of her major novels were not the exploration of a new set of characters in new situations. Pym is no more repetitive or autobiographical than most major novelists.

The three novels that follow, the unfinished war novel 'Amanda Wraye' (1939), *Crampton Hodnet* (written 1939–40), and the spy novel, 'So Very Secret', begun in September 1941, already show Pym distancing herself from the preoccupations of the previous novels, varying setting and mode, and responding to the greater awareness of history forced on her by the war. Pym's earlier ignorance of political and historical realities is evident from her letters and journals. Though her trips to Germany were made during the rise of National Socialism, she seems to have been unaware of anything sinister about the development. Hazel Holt quotes this passage from a letter as evidence that she was 'really rather naive':

> There was much merriment – shouting and singing too – English and German songs. We sang *God Save the King* and *Deutschland Uber Alles* – that rather worried Friedbert, although I couldn't understand why. (*A Very Private Eye*, p. 13)

In the first version of *Some Tame Gazelle* there is a running joke about how Belinda is always knitting objects for the poor Nazis who have been overthrown by a revolution and are now in exile somewhere in Africa. The limits of Pym's sense of domestic politics are suggested by her cheerfully naïve responses to the Hunger Marches of 1934, and by an account of a day out with Harvey in a friend's Bentley: 'We saw some cottages for the poor, aged and impotent but somehow it was difficult to imagine that either of us would ever be those things' (*A Very Private Eye*, pp. 69, 70).

The novels of the war years show a deepening and enlarging of Pym's sense of history, a sense which, in varying degrees, informs all the subsequent works. One of the criteria by which we judge a novelist major is the ability to register larger historical processes; to give us, in the texture and structure of a work, an account of the relation of the individual life to the larger forces. Pym's novels are, as has been suggested, consciously and ironically posed as minor, but the reader misses a great deal if he or she takes that pose at face value (like a male failing to perceive the significance of a woman's understated remarks in a conversation). Indirection is often part of the art of representing history. Thackeray in *Vanity Fair*, for instance, does not directly represent the great events of the Napoleonic Wars but suggests their indirect effects on the lives of individuals. Pym's indirection is still more subtle. Her characters are often consciously indifferent to anything but the private, or extremely naïve about the larger world, or only vaguely aware that they represent a way of life that is being affected by history. History, in a sense, eludes them, or they it, and history is an elusive presence in the novels. Nevertheless it is a presence. In her sure but indirect presentation of the relation of lives to historical developments, the gathering accretions of loss and displacement, Pym catches the essential movement and texture of one phase of English history. The relation minor–major must therefore be put in question, for not only does Pym suggest that minor events in minor lives have an indirect relation to the major, but her historical subject is, in fact, how something major – Britain – became minor.

Pym's growing awareness of the public world was affected by her relationship with the Oxford undergraduate. He appears as 'Hughie Otway' in 'Beatrice Wyatt' and in the short unfinished draft of the novel 'Something to Remember' (1940), and as Stephen in *Crampton Hodnet*. Members of his family also appear in 'Amanda Wraye' and the spy novel 'So Very Secret'. The Oxford undergraduate was Julian Amery, whose father, Leopold Amery, was a member of Parliament for over thirty years and held important government posts, including First Lord of the Admiralty and Secretary of State for Commonwealth and Dominion Affairs. Julian Amery had made a name for himself reporting on the Spanish Civil War. He subsequently went to Yugoslavia, became press attaché at the British Embassy, and worked for British intelligence. He later married Catherine, the daughter of the future Prime Minister Harold Macmillan, and became a member of Parliament on the right of the British Conservative Party. Pym characterises the father of 'Hughie Otway' as a pompous and empty politician; the mother as the victim of a family in which the private has been sacrificed to the public; and the son as vain and ambitious. The family is wealthy, fashionable, with a home in Belgrave Square: of a class, it is implied, for which a plain young woman such as Pym, from the merely respectable middle classes, would lack real significance. Pym's attitude was doubtless in part formed by personal pique, but it is none the less significant. Like Jane Austen and Trollope before her, Pym perceived a difference between the national grandees and the decently genteel, and treated the former with irony and mistrust. There were, however, great differences between her situation and that of her predecessors. Austen could imagine Fanny Price and her Edmund regenerating Mansfield Park; Trollope could look to the solid strata of country gentry. Pym's nice people, on the other hand, are always represented as fading in social significance, decent people adrift from the centres of power.

As a single woman, Pym was distant from her 'natural' political representatives. The kind of position she could occupy is nicely suggested by a passage in 'So Very Secret':

> As I am unmarried I have no very great respect for men – I do not think they are so wonderful as all that. They make a hopeless mess of running the Country and I do not believe any of our politicians would be able to do the blackout in his own house unaided. At least I daresay Mr Bevin and Mr Morrison could. Agnes says she is never going to vote Conservative again and I am almost inclined to agree with her except that I keep wondering whatever would father say – and then of course Hughie is a Conservative MP. Tradition dies hard among English spinsters especially where politics are mixed with remembrance of a past love.
>
> (MS Pym 12/1–4, fo. 20)

This sentimental attachment without belief to conservatism – or simply the old ways – is far from the stance of the more-conservative-than-the conservative woman most conspicuously represented today by Margaret Thatcher. Pym's position allows her to register both the new and disturbing developments in society and the falling-short of niceness and human adequacy of the social and political establishment.

The unfinished war novel, based on the early or 'phoney war' period, 'Amanda Wraye' (MS Pym 8), is Pym's first conscious attempt to suggest the feeling of real and unreal connections between private and public worlds. A loose manuscript sheet headed 'Plan so far' includes the sentences:

In General. the atmosphere of a weekend crisis but war won't come
And a clear setting of the characters and their circumstances

The novel is more successful in its evocation of the atmosphere of a crisis that will not quite come than in its representation of characters and their relations; it is perhaps too conscious an attempt to write a new kind of novel, as though Pym had not yet learnt to orchestrate relation to the deeper historical movement, or gives too much over to it. The most memorable parts of 'Amanda Wraye' are passages such as this:

there were petunias in Mandy's window box. Mandy felt almost happy as she looked at them, she loved flowers. And then she saw the air raid trenches dug in the square gardens and she suddenly realised that they had a meaning too. A wave of desolation swept over her and she saw Eaton Square a mess of smouldering ruins. Would they all crowd into the trench of sodden clay, like a newly dug grave, she and Lyall, the Calyxes, the Vicar, Lord Stamp, old Lady Holland, the idea of it suddenly became funny.   (fo. 4)

The movement of feeling from sentiment to desolation to satire is attractive. The same range of responses come into the representation of the feelings of the young woman Flora. Flora is unsure whether to be broken-hearted at the departure of her love to war or not, unsure even whether he is her love. The parting is unsatisfactory to her, but she is pleased to be able to arrange his photograph amongst the other objects in her room. There then follows a subtle and evocative scene which depicts Flora lying in the bath in a blacked-out bathroom:

This war was going to be the end of everything.
    She felt a curious peace stealing over her, it was so dark and warm. There was something soothing about the finality of her thoughts –
    'Flora, are you asleep?' came Jane's voice at the door.

Flora started. She had been getting very drowsy . . .

'Remember Aunt Bella,' said Jane. 'Are you getting out?'

'Yes, I am.' Flora climbed slowly out of the bath. Aunt Bella went to sleep in the bath and her head slipped down into the water and she drowned, she thought stupidly. She was an old woman of eighty something. Flora could see her lying still and peaceful in the cool cloudy water, in the old fashioned bath embedded in mahogany. It must be a nice way to die, rather inconvenient for other people, but peaceful. Not bloody or violent like dying in a war would be. (fo. 50)

Flora is curiously drawn to this strangely preserved image of the past, a reaction at odds with her cool, unemotional, modern daylight self.

The narrator of 'So Very Secret' remarks that 'I think we all look back to the Victorian Age now with a sort of longing. It was so safe and comfortable for our class and if there were wars they were fought decently by professional soldiers and abroad' (MS Pym 12/1–4, fo. 44v). The imaginative use of the Victorian past is one of the immediate products of Pym's awakening sense of the larger historical scene. In one of her most successful unpublished short stories, 'Goodbye Balkan Capital', set during the war, a private relation to the Victorian past is linked, in a development of Flora's situation, to a detachment from present emotions and a curious feeling of freedom. The story again owes something to Pym's relationship with Amery. A woman's self-seeking ex-lover has become a diplomat. She has imagined him fleeing a Balkan capital before the onslaught of the Axis powers, but finds, when she reads his obituary in *The Times*, that he has all along been in England. There follows a passage in which the heroine reflects on her personal relation to a Victorian past and her detachment from the socialist future, but also, more complexly, on her detachment from the ambitions and world of her dead lover. The result is to establish her freedom and choice:

She found it hard to look forward to the future and a New Social Order, when there had been so much happiness in the past, the bad old days, as she had heard them called. Surely *they* (by whom she usually meant people like Mr Herbert Morrison and Mr Ernest Bevin) would leave her that, her

Victorian paperweight, with its bright and simple design of flowers? Perhaps she had already been punished for her self-indulgent dreaming by her disillusionment about Crispin. No dramatic 'Goodbye, Balkan Capital!' but a quiet death in a safe part of England. It was even possible that *her* end might be more violent and exciting than his.

Why, she thought, when the siren went that evening, I might get killed by a bomb! And yet that would not be right. It was always Crispin who had the dramatic adventures, and after all these years Laura did not want it to be any different. In life or death people are very much what we like to think them. Laura knew that she might search in vain for the Oxfordshire churchyard among the new graves with their sodden wreathes to find Crispin's. . . . But it would be easy in the Balkans, the dangerous places. There would always be something of him there.   (MS Pym 92)

The conclusion has a fine irony. In the images in this and in the 'Amanda Wraye' passage of a sentiment, even a self, preserved or enshrined – the old lady in the bath, the Victorian paperweight – we have a glimpse not only of fidelity but also of *form*. The feeling of power to range and create in the latter passage, though ironically limited, suggests a new order of achieved power and confidence. It can be seen that the war and the working-out of the 'Hughie Otway' relationship provided a stimulus to a new phase in Pym's writing, a dislocation and a new access of energy; involved in this was an attachment to an ideal past social order, and a detachment from its present representatives.

The immediate fruit of these developments was *Crampton Hodnet*, Pym's last Oxford novel, and certainly her most successful novel of this period. The Victorian past is a strong presence in it, largely because of the descriptions of North Oxford (a wealthy suburb of Oxford, immediately north of the colleges, which is distinguished by the large homes built for Oxford dons in the latter half of the nineteenth century after the university permitted dons to marry). It begins,

It was a wet Sunday afternoon in North Oxford at the beginning of October. The laurel bushes which bordered the path leading to Leamington Lodge, Banbury Road, were

dripping with rain. A few sodden chrysanthemums, dahlias
and zinnias drooped in the flower-beds on the lawn. The
house had been built in the sixties of the last century, of
yellowish brick, with a gabled roof and narrow Gothic
windows set in frames of ornamental stonework. A long red
and blue-stained-glass window looked onto a landing halfway
up the pitch-pine staircase, and there were panels of the
same glass let into the front door, giving an ecclesiastical
effect, so that, except for a glimpse of unlikely lace curtains,
the house might have been a theological college. It seemed
very quiet now.   (ch. 1)

Imagery of the emotions and the spirit – the flowers, the rain,
the religiose architecture – are taken up into the solid
respectabilities of established wealth and social standing; the
glimpse of femininity, the lace curtains, like the hem of a
petticoat, appears incongruous. The house is the home of the
elderly spinster Maude Doggett, also of her plain and no-longer
young companion, Jessica Morrow. These two characters are
familiar to Pym readers from their appearance in *Jane and
Prudence*, which, though written later than *Crampton Hodnet*, was
published earlier. There are important differences in the manner
of presentation of the two Jessicas, however. Jessica Morrow is
here the principal point of view in the novel, not, as she is in
Jane and Prudence, a character whose furtive detachment and
private arrangement with her emotional and sexual needs
remain unfathomable to all. The difference between the two
Jessicas – the name perhaps deriving from Shylock's neglected
daughter – is seen in the fact that the principal event for the
Jessica of *Crampton Hodnet* is her rejection of the proposal by a
handsome young curate who she is sure does not love her:
'Even Miss Morrow's standards were higher than that, so high,
indeed, that she feared she would never marry now. For she
wanted love' (ch. 10). She finds a curiously satisfying personal
freedom in the life of the plain, single and neglected woman:
'That was the best of drab clothes. One could be a nature
worshipper without fear of soiling one's dress' (ch. 16). In *Jane
and Prudence*, on the other hand, Jessica Morrow entraps the
shallow if handsome Fabian Driver into marriage.
Nevertheless, the fact that the Jessica of *Crampton Hodnet*
could become the character in *Jane and Prudence* suggests the

cramped and repressed experience of the heroine, the effort of detachment and self-subduing, and the cost of achieved form and distance in this novel. There are a couple of scenes in which Jessica appears in Miss Doggett's drawing-room in what Miss Doggett regards as the incongruity of the clothes and make-up of an attractive and significant woman. But the sense of incongruity is not only Miss Doggett's, for there is something disturbing about Jessica's appearances and her subsequent retreats to erase or remove the signs of her desire. It is as though what she has done is painfully revealing, hurtful and embarrassing. This sense persists despite the repeated assurances and demonstrations that Jessica is coolly self-possessed. In this respect, there is also a disquieting element in Jessica's relation to the bullying and crushing Miss Doggett, for, rather than producing any revolt in Jessica, it seems to provide her with a kind of reassurance, in so far as it relieves her from the aspiration to a self and any possible illusions. Jessica is in fact dependent on this stalwart representative of North Oxford, as a certain kind of emotionally ill young woman seeks to obscure herself in her mother's world:

> Miss Morrow walked meekly along by Miss Doggett's side, a comforting neutral thing, without form or sex. There was something so restful in being somebody whose presence made no difference one way or the other. (ch. 17)

From her position of chameleon-like security, Jessica can survey a world of romantic folly with little sympathy or risk. There is a definite achievement in this evocation of the adjacent, and, in their way, complementary lives of these two women, of the atmosphere, furnishings, and rituals of behaviour of their world, but its centrality also marks the limits of the possible emotional flow of the novel, the comedy of which has, as a result, a slightly cruel and even bitter tone.

The novel runs in parallel three Oxford love stories. There is the handsome and weak young curate, Stephen Lattimer, Miss Doggett's lodger, who, seeking some security, proposes to Jessica, is rejected, and at the novel's end falls in love banally and properly while on holiday. There is Anthea Cleveland, pretty young daughter of an Oxford don, who falls in love with the ambitious and vain Stephen Beddoes, son of the British

Ambassador at Warsaw, Lord Beddoes: Anthea's heart is broken, but it mends just as rapidly. Finally there is her father, Francis Cleveland, who feels neglected by his busy and practical wife, and who falls for a pretty young undergraduate with the delightful name of Barbara Bird. Romantic love is thus treated as unreliable, incongruous and embarrassing, and of these stories Francis Cleveland's is the richest in these qualities: scenes of stolen meetings and embraces observed by passing elderly colleagues have a wincing comedy. Neither Francis nor Barbara has a very genuine sentiment for the other. She has indulged the conventional idealisation of a teacher; is disturbed when Francis responds; tries, equally conventionally, to live up to her emotion; and then at the critical moment, retreats. Francis himself has very much sentimentalised this inadequate love object, and his feeling for her is much mixed with peevish resentment towards his wife and family. The tone of the affair and the position of Jessica Morrow in these complications is caught in the scene of Francis's proclamation to his wife, or, rather, to the intrusive and interfering Miss Doggett and his other neighbours:

> 'I love Miss Bird and she loves me!' he said hotly. 'It is just that, since you insist on knowing.' And then he went out of the room and dramatically slammed the door.
> Why had he said Miss Bird? Why not Barbara? thought Miss Morrow, missing the real significance of his statement and concentrating only on trivialities. 'I love Miss Bird and she loves me!' . . . Miss Morrow felt her mouth curling at the corners.   (ch. 17)

The outburst is funny, but it would be easier to laugh if we were not invited to share Miss Morrow's smirk. Despite the unreality of his declaration, Francis makes an attempt at going through with his decision to run off to France. They do not get far, for at a Dover hotel reality and North Oxford close in on them:

> She stood in the lounge, nervously twisting her hands and looking round her with some agitation. She saw that the room was decorated with stiff palms in brass pots and that, grouped in a corner, as if for artistic effect, were a number of

old people reading the newspapers. They looked as if they had been left there for many years and abandoned. Or perhaps they were people who at some time long past had intended to go abroad and had then either not wanted to or forgotten all about it, so that they had stayed here ever since, like fossils petrified in stone.   (ch. 20)

Barbara flees to a friend, and Francis is defeated: 'After a while the old people roused themselves and went upstairs to sleep again. Francis followed them without a murmur. Indeed, he now felt himself to be one of them' (ibid.).

It is as though Francis has been made to come back, unwillingly, to a lumber room, and in the handling of this part of the novel there may be a last working-out of animosity about Harvey's marriage (in 'Beatrice Wyatt', before the unconvincing reunion of Beatrice and Henry, Beatrice had reflected, 'It was difficult to feel melancholy regrets about somebody who seems to be getting more of a dull Don every time one met him – giving lectures on Piers Plowman and growing a bit thin on top!' – MS 6/1–3, fo. 103). At any rate, in *Crampton Hodnet* the Victorian past is not at a poignant distance, as it was in Flora's vision, but is a solid and even vengeful present:

'No, I do not think you will find any change and decay in Leamington Lodge,' said Miss Doggett, smiling.
And Miss Morrow was inclined to agree with her.
(ch. 23)

However, as has been suggested, Pym's identification with North Oxford was at some cost of self-expression and sentiment, and there is another vision of the Victorian past, at once more humorous and more freed for sentiment, in the novel. In a work much influenced by Betjeman it is the most Betjemanesque passage:

Miss Morrow always enjoyed these summer evenings. The effect of light and sunshine on the heavy furniture, the dark covers, the silver-table, the Bavarian engravings, even on the photograph of Canon Tottle, gave her the idea that there might be a life beyond this, where even the contents of Miss Doggett's drawing-room might be bathed in heavenly radiance. It was a confused and certainly quite wrong idea but a pleasing and comforting one, to imagine the whole of North Oxford, its houses and inhabitants, lifted just as they were into heaven, where all the objects would be the same in themselves but invested with a different meaning from that which they had on earth. They would all be dear, treasured things because they would be part of the heavenly atmosphere. It was not difficult, Miss Morrow thought, to imagine that heaven might be something like North Oxford. Certainly if there were any buildings there the architecture might well be Gothic – and why not the Victorian Gothic of North Oxford rather than the thirteenth-century Gothic of a continental cathedral? (ch. 12)

There is an enshrining, embalming quality about this, and, not surprisingly, Miss Morrow finds it difficult to imagine the worldly Miss Doggett in her Victorian heaven.

Pym's feelings, the new mobility in her life, and the events of the war, were conspiring together to open up for her interiors and landscapes of fidelity and distance. In 1939 she wrote in her diary,

What is the heart? A damp cave with things growing in it, mysterious secret plants of love or whatever you like. Or a dusty lumber room full of junk. Or a neat orderly place like a desk with a place for everything and everything in its place.

Something might be starting now that would linger on through many years – dying sometimes and then coming back again, like a twinge of rheumatism in the winter, so that you suddenly felt it in your knee when you were nearing the top of a long flight of stairs.

A Great Love that was unrequited might well be like that.

So many places where one has enjoyed oneself are no more – notably Stewart's in Oxford – shops are pulled down, houses in ruins, people in their marble vaults whom one had thought to be still living. One looks through the window in a house in Belgravia and sees right through its uncurtained space into a conservatory with a dusty palm, a room without furniture and discoloured spaces on the walls where pictures of ancestors once hung. One passes a house in Bayswater with steep steps and sees a coffin being carried out.

(*A Very Private Eye*, pp. 127–8)

Pym's spy novel, 'So Very Secret', the last of the novels of the war years, opens as a village comedy in the *Some Tame Gazelle* vein, but, as its unconvincing and unexciting plot develops, it takes its middle-aged heroine to a succession of scenes that encapsulate the imagery and experiences of these years. She goes first to a sinister house in North Oxford where she is drugged and imprisoned but from which she escapes. She then follows her creator to war-time London, where the moments of perception are as intense as anything in the diaries:

> Here in this train between Oxford and London time was standing still – the sleeping soldier opposite me, the airman and his mother in the other corner were all immortalised for me into this time of remembering. I shall never forget them. (MS Pym 12/1–4, fo. 93v)

In London she goes first to the West End, where she enters into the house of the Otways, gets a glimpse of the pompous meaninglessness of Otway senior's political world, and slips out unrecognised. Then she confronts London's Victorian past:

> Maida Vale <was> ᴵˢ wide and somehow *noble*, I always think <though it is a decayed nobility> ᴵⁿ ˢᵖᶦᵗᵉ ᵒᶠ with the crowds and dust and the sunshine. But now with the ruins here and there the nobility seemed to have come back. The great family homes, built for Victorians with large gardens, and barred nursery windows are relics of an age we like to remember. Here was a house painted turquoise blue and another called Mizpah. The Lord watch between me and thee while we are separated one from another. (fo. 95)

On the facing page of the manuscript she added for insertion the sentences 'It comes so suddenly out of the squalor of the Edgeware Road' and 'Their ruins might have a kind if grandeur like Ancient Greece and Rome' (fo. 94v). A curious scene of a meeting with a sympathetic prostitute (a fallen and shamed woman) follows: a moment of healing. The plot then pursues its way across England, picking up characters who were to appear in the first of the post-war novels, *Excellent Women* (Father Julian and his sister, Mildred). A phase of feeling was 'complete', and for the longest period in her adult life, at the height of the war, Pym ceased to write fiction.

The novels of these years point to a number of facts pertinent to an appreciation of the view of English history in Pym's fiction. She is, in her direct way, the chronicler of the end of a phase of her civilisation, of the home view of the end of Empire. Her temperament and experience made it impossible for her to identify strongly with the assertive representatives of her class, though she was also cut off from many of the developments that can loosely be associated with their socialist alternative. Her attachment was rather to an ideal image of the past of her class, which, unaligned with that class's real continuing power, found images of its allegiance in relics of the Victorian age. There is an unpublished and undated story (which exists in two manuscript versions), 'The Rich Man in his Castle' (MS Pym 92). A young couple, tourists, come across a Victorian monument. A flashback tells us that the monument is to the daughter of a wealthy and aristocratic Victorian family who, influenced by a man of lower social standing, visited the poor during a typhoid epidemic and as a result died. As the story returns to the present, the male of the couple remarks that the Victorians believed in

> The rich man at his castle
> The poor man at his gate

but the young woman with him, though she has not heard the story of the memorial, thinks (though she does not say it) that 'Death doesn't distinguish between rich and poor', and avers, 'Of course they were *good*, the Victorians, in a way we don't really understand now.' This is a very different view of the Victorians from that popularised in the era of Mrs Thatcher, and in Pym's post-war novels the adequate image of this emotional and spiritual allegiance is not the great Victorian house, but London's apparently rather pointless Victorian churches.

3

The Comedies

At the height of the war Pym ceased for a time to write fiction. When she began again it was in a different world. It was not only the war which made a break with her Oswestry and Oxford life. In September 1945 Pym's mother died, and the following year her father remarried. The world of her childhood had passed away. From 1946, Pym's home was London, and the novels of the next period are, with the partial exception of *Jane and Prudence*, London novels.

This is the period of her greatest creativity and, arguably, her greatest literary achievement. Between 1949 and 1955, she wrote four fine comic novels, *Excellent Women* (published 1952), *Jane and Prudence* (1953), *Less than Angels* (1955) and *A Glass of Blessings* (1958); after 1955 a less assured period in her writing begins, which is discussed in the next chapter. It is a sign of Pym's development as a writer that the novels of this period are significantly less autobiographical than the novels prior to them, or, rather, since autobiographical elements can be discovered in them all, they are less confined by their author's needs, and more various in their imagining. Though the worlds of these novels in a degree interconnect, and certain characters appear or are mentioned in more than one of them, each is a fresh conception, developing a distinct poetic texture and set of relations and possibilities.

Similarly, though there are certain common elements that enable us to discern a characteristically Pymian female point of view, the heroines of these works, Mildred, Jane and Prudence, Catherine and Wilmet, are all distinct individuals. Between them, they explore a range of possibilities open to the young-to-middle-aged woman, married or single, making her way with a large measure of financial and mental independence in the England of the post-war era. The lively engagement with life of these witty, appealing heroines is one of the great attractions of these novels. Though memory and fidelity are themes of Pym's novels, and though her heroines are often baffled or disturbed by the new social conditions and *mores*, these novels have a flavour of adventure and an openness that removes them from any preoccupation with the past. Pym does not write in the recollective mode, and, though they approach it in a sideways fashion, the heroines of these novels are ready for the life of their time.

In 1946 Barbara Pym began as a research assistant under Professor Daryll Forde, the distinguished anthropologist, at the International African Institute. Anthropology and anthropologists appear as a subject in a number of her novels. Pym usually adopts the point of view of the outsider, affecting an incomprehension of its terms and subject matter which renders anthropology a pedantic jargon (somewhat like scholarly literary studies). Only in *Less than Angels* is the reality of the country in which anthropological study is conducted recognised. She thus frees herself to observe anthropology as a field for ambition and egoism at home. It is an area where men are observed by women, who in turn perform the unrewarding and unacknowledged tasks of editing, proof-reading and compiling indexes. Pym does introduce successful female anthropologists – Helen Napier in *Excellent Women* and the admirable Esther Clovis – but her central characters, whose points of view she adopts, are not career women. They hold the traditional female occupations, working as librarians, office workers, charity workers and housewives. This is perhaps a limitation in her work, but it is underwritten in Pym by a deep doubt as to the value of the pursuit of a career by either a man or a woman. It is not just that she perceives that a rather pointless activity may sustain an unjustified egoism. Pym seems to feel that we are truer to ourselves when we recognise our modest needs, desires and significance.

In a short piece in *The Times* written late in her life, Pym argued that the practice of the novelist can be compared to that of the anthropologist ('In Defence of the Novel: Why You Shouldn't Have to Wait until the Afternoon', *The Times*, 22 February 1978, p. 18). Numbers of critics have taken up the comparison. Marilyn Butler (1982), for instance, argued that what separates Pym's narrative technique from that of predecessors such as Jane Austen is a certain detached cataloguing of details of appearance and of events which she shares with the functional school of anthropologists. Something must be allowed for this argument, but Pym's doubts about anthropology and detached observation are more striking. She frequently plays on the correspondence between the observing novelist and the observing anthropologist, but most typically she represents the former as practising something like what Lawrence called knowing-in-togetherness, whereas the latter adopts a mode of knowing-in-apartness. Her most powerful and searching anthropological novel, *Less than Angels*, gives a fierce twist to this relation, and her last novel, *A Few Green Leaves*, has an anthropologist as heroine, but the point there is that the distance adopted in the heroine's career has emptied her life of involvement and meaning. Perhaps the most balanced view is that Pym saw a correspondence between, on the one hand, an aspect of herself and her practice as a novelist, and, on the other, the anthropologist and his or her work – not that she underwrote the correspondence.

A further function of anthropology in her novels is that it enables her to introduce codes of imagery from non-English life which enable her to dramatise a deeper movement of feelings than appears on the surface of her genteel English world, and in *Less than Angels* and in a number of her later novels, the limitations of English life are very much part of her subject.

Excellent Women

The manuscript notebook for *Excellent Women* (MS Pym 13) is headed by the title 'A Full Life'. A second notebook (MS Pym 14), which contains a draft of the first seven chapters, has at its beginning the note

> No Life of One's own –
> Spinster without ties – inquisitive, willing to help others
> An onlooker sees most of the game etc.

Excellent Women presents the life of an onlooker, moving somewhere between a full life and no life of her own.

The first of the notebooks contains an outline of the story as Pym first conceived it. It is worth quoting in its entirety as it

allows us to see both the high degree of artistic certainty with
which Pym began and also the changes by which she refined
her initial conception:

> In brief it is the story of a woman – a pleasant humorous
> spinster in the middle thirties – who gets continually
> embroiled in other people's affairs the set up as is follows –
> She lives in a flat in a house (somewhere like Pimlico) which
> has two or three flats – not self contained. She first meets
> Mrs Mogden (Eleanor) when she is carrying down the
> rubbish. Mrs M married to a naval officer who has been in
> Naples, moves in. They have a house in the country adjoining
> the one where the spinster's father was a vicar. Think the flat
> rather awful but the best thing they can do – they have some
> 'nice things'. While her husband was in Naples Mrs M was
> doing anthropological work (in Nigeria perhaps) with a fellow
> anthropologist. Mr M has met a nice Wren whom he wants
> to marry so he tries to divorce his wife citing the
> anthropologist. The spinster gets involved – after getting to
> know them first she is asked down to their cottage and made
> to write letters about furniture. In addition she is much
> concerned with church matters – the vicar (Fr Somebody)
> lives with his sister in a large vicarage. He wants to get
> married and the sister, feeling she is turned out, comes to the
> spinster. Again the spinster must negotiate about objects and belongings.
> The anthropologist, in the meantime, is offered some
> position – but questions are asked about his relationship with
> Mrs M.
> In the end, I should think, you have Mrs M, the vicar's
> sister and the spinster all living somewhat uncomfortably
> together. Until a relative writes to the spinster and begs for
> her services as a companion.

There are a number of differences between this summary and
the novel as we have it. The restriction of the action of the
novel to London gives it a uniform atmosphere. Helena Napier
(the 'Mrs M' of the draft) is the active disrupter of her
marriage, not Rocky ('Mr M'); Rocky is thus released to
become the more sympathetic comic character he is in the
novel, and with that release there is space for the spinster,

Mildred, to develop feelings for him. The clergyman, Julian Mallory, in the end rejects his fiancée, not his sister. The general effect of these changes is to make the events and motives of the characters less crude; we have a more typically Pymian, and perhaps more adult, non-event. The revisions also serve to bring Mildred more to the novel's centre: the choice of a first-person narrative is made early in the notes that follow this summary.

The change wrought in British society by the war is evident in *Excellent Women*. Some of the characters worship in one aisle of a church which has been bombed: "We had made our way through the ruins, where torn-down wall tablets and an occasional urn or cherub's head were stacked in heaps, and where, incongruous in the middle of so much desolation, we had come upon a little grey woman heating a saucepan of coffee on a Primus stove' (ch. 6). On the other hand the new impersonal modernity is imaged in a scene in a self-service cafeteria: 'The room was enormous, like something in a nightmare. . . . a file of people moved in through a door at one end and formed a long line fenced off from the main part of the room by a brass rail.' The brass rail and line, by recalling details of Communion in church, suggest a desacralised space.

Jumble sales and the tombstones in a churchyard visited during a school reunion add to this sense of a broken inheritance and recall the images of lumber rooms and a ruined Victorian world in the unpublished novels. Mildred Lathbury, the narrator of the novel, has a rented room, with shared bathroom, but her room is furnished with the good Victorian things left her by her clergyman father. Rockingham Napier, the naval officer whose arrival with his wife in the flat below is destined to disturb Mildred's life, owns similar things, 'Victorian paper weights and snowstorms, very much like those I had on my own mantelpiece upstairs' (ch. 1), but they are collected, not inherited – an amusing taste overlaying an essential restlessness and lack of values. Rocky does not attend church regularly; expressing his restlessness at the crisis of his marriage, he complains about Matthew Arnold's 'Yes! In the sea of life enisled', favourite lines of Pym's; flings down Mildred's father's volume of Arnold; and mocks women's fidelity and the phrase *Semper Fidelis*, which was Mildred's school motto: 'it might be the title of a Victorian painting of a huge dog of the Landseer

variety' (ch. 15; an image recalled in *A Few Green Leaves*). In
this novel, Pym puts both her character, Mildred, and her
image stock at risk.

The risk is desire and the exposure of the desiring self.
Mildred Lathbury likes to think she is her own woman – 'I
valued my independence very dearly' (ch. 2) – and that she
has few illusions: 'Let me hasten to add that I am not at all like
Jane Eyre, who must have given hope to so many plain women
who tell their stories in the first person' (ch. 1). Of course,
we all, plain and handsome alike, tell our stories in the first
person, and the story of that person is very much the story of
desire. Mildred, however, wishes to be in control, and believes
she is; she is a clergyman's daughter, has worked in the
Censorship during the war, and now works for a charity for
dispossessed gentle persons, a life that has taught her scrutiny
and suspicion, though also the habit of repression.

Mildred's chief quality is a dry wit, of which she herself is
often the subject: 'I know myself to be capable of dealing with
most of the stock situations or even the great moments of life –
birth, marriage, death, the successful jumble sale, the garden
fête spoilt by bad weather' (ch. 1). This wit sets the tone of the
early parts of the novel: looking at Helena Napier's books,
Mildred observes, 'Many of them seemed to be of an obscure
scientific nature, and there was a pile of journals with green
covers which bore the rather stark and surprising title of *Man*. I
wondered what they could be about' (ibid.). Sharp recognitions
are of its essence: 'The burden of keeping three people in toilet
paper seemed to me rather a heavy one' (ibid.). Or of a meal of
macaroni cheese at the rector's and his sister's: 'Not enough
salt, or perhaps *no* salt, I thought, as I ate the macaroni. And
not really enough cheese' (ch. 2). Which does not leave a great
deal to say for it. The irony extends to others, for Mildred is an
observant person – 'people do not always realise that cleaning a
bath properly can be quite hard work' (ch. 3) – but the chief
satisfaction is in self-recognition:

> I remembered girlhood dances where one had stayed there
> [the ladies'] too long, though never long enough to last out
> the dance for which one hadn't a partner. I didn't suppose
> Helena had ever known that, and yet it was in its way quite a
> deep experience.   (ch. 10)

This detached view of the self comes under increasing pressure as the first person emerges, driving the wit to a slightly hectic eccentricity:

> 'Oh they have a knack of catching a man. . . .'
> 'Like mending a fuse,' I suggested. . . . (ch. 13)

And, in her disappointment and irritation, Mildred can become almost Dickensian in her self-presentation:

> 'Is she fatherless too?'
> 'Yes, she is an orphan,' he said solemnly.
> 'Well, of course, a lot of people over thirty are orphans. I am myself,' I said briskly. 'In fact I was an orphan in my twenties.' (ch. 15)

Mildred is not jealous in this case (though she is thought to be) but we can see the witty, dry estimate of self and others slipping towards bitterness under the pressure of unrequited emotion. It is because she is so much her own woman and yet so vulnerable that Mildred is sensed to have a capacity for pain: she has a kind of stiffness, an almost ungainly resistance, that gives feeling a peculiar capacity to hurt. When, at the height of her emotional turbulence, she insists on buying a lipstick luridly called 'Hawaiian fire', we are reminded of a similar gesture made by Jessica Morrow in *Crampton Hodnet*.

A determined self-knowledge that is also a repression leaves one open to subsequent humiliating self-knowledge and to the easy condescension and pity of others. The opening paragraphs of the novel suggests how very vulnerable to another interpretation Mildred is:

> 'Ah, you ladies! Always on the spot when there's something happening!' The voice belonged to Mr Mallett, one of our churchwardens, and its roguish tone made me start guiltily, almost as if I had no right to be discovered outside my own front door. . . .
> I suppose an unmarried woman just over thirty, who lives alone and has no apparent ties, must expect to find herself involved or interested in other people's business, and if she is also a clergyman's daughter then one might really say that there is no hope for her. (ch. 1)

Mildred's dry wit, re-establishes her and rebuffs Mr Mallett's tired masculine attitude, but it is, nevertheless, self-deceiving: she is not simply interested in other people's business (self-knowledge) but interested in her own (self-deception). Thus the scene of exposure to bluff male interpretaton (its concomitants – plain, spinster, needs a man – need not be spelt out) with which the novel opens reveals Mildred's blind side and dangerous vulnerability. Mallett, is, after all, right in his innuendo: within a short time, Mildred's head is filled with Rocky Napier and his situation, needs and feelings, almost as though she, not Helena, were his wife: 'I might have to go down and open the door. He would certainly have no latch-key and he might not have had supper. I now began to feel almost agitated' (ch. 4).

The unconventional and unstable nature of the Napiers' marriage, spring, and the opening out of post-war life (Helena is a career woman; Rocky is returned from unonerous naval duties in Italy) serve to excite Mildred's 'first person', to awaken in her an irritable restlessness with old friends and desireless attachments, unexpected bursts of emotion and declaration:

> I suppose it must have been the Nuits St Georges or the spring day or the intimate atmosphere of the restaurant, but I heard myself to my horror, murmuring something about Rocky Napier being just the kind of person I should have liked for myself.   (ch. 8)

The threat lies in the conventionality of Mildred's romantic idea. Rocky Napier, facile, easy-going, charming, is one of Pym's great male characters, a splendid comic rendering of a stereotypical female object of desire, easily, even modestly, aware he is that. His relationship with Helena is disturbed by her failure to be many of the conventional, even reasonable, things a wife might be expected to be; by his flirtations and affairs in Italy (we learn he has kept an Italian mistress); and by Helena's pursuit of a career and her fellow anthropologist, Everard Bone. Helena is a nicely observed type, an early model, as it were, of the independent career woman, who requires masculine indulgence to pursue her career and pursues it largely in terms of love objects. In her, Rocky, like Mildred, has been surprised by modernity (like Mildred, he understands nothing of anthropology 'I shall let it flow over me', he remarks of the lecture to which his wife takes him); hence he finds Mildred a comfortable supporter, for she has all the traditional female virtues Helena has forgotten or, more likely, never knew. The degree of his appreciation of Mildred awakens in her memories and hopes of desire, but also, since there is no possibility of his taking a reciprocal romantic interest in her, a wretched weariness. At the end of one chapter, Mildred remembers her rejection by her only previous love:

> Perhaps high-principled young men were more cruel in these matters because less experienced. I am sure that Rocky would have done it much more kindly.
>
> I got up stiffly, for I had been crouching uncomfortably on the floor. I bundled the letters and photographs back and decided that it would be more profitable to make tea and cut out my dress.   (ch. 13)

Rocky would make a kind end of one. The image of Mildred crouching in the cupboard anticipates a moment of Prudence Bates's desolation in *Jane and Prudence*, and the suggestion of a kind strong lover putting one out of one's pain anticipates details in two of Pym's later novels, *The Sweet Dove Died* and *Quartet in Autumn*.

Rocky has spent his war entertaining Wren officers in Italy, and the kind of woman who falls for Rocky is represented for Mildred by those anonymous Wrens. They stand for a response in herself she does not wish to admit, and, more complexly, for a role in which she feels incongruous – that of the desiring woman. As her involvement with Rocky progresses, the thought of the Wrens is repressed – 'It wasn't till afterwards that I remembered the Wren officers' (ch. 8) – but their return, carrying with it a humiliating self-recognition and confession, is inevitable:

> Once more, perhaps for the last time, I saw the Wren officers huddled together in an awkward like group on the terrace of the Admiral's villa. Rocky's kindness must surely have meant a great deal to them at that moment and perhaps some of them would never forget it as long as they lived.   (ch. 24)

But, as her use of the figures of the Wrens suggest, in coming
into her first person, Mildred is coming into a third-person role
in Rocky's life. He is, after all, married, and neither he nor
Helena seriously wishes to be otherwise. Mildred functions for
them in the classic third-person role of confidante, go-between,
mediator, arranger. Her duties include helping Helena move
out, helping move Rocky's furniture to a country cottage, then
writing to him on behalf of Helena when she seeks a
reconciliation. In a final scene in the flat they are now leaving
together, Rocky and Helena have a last drink with Mildred,
and in their uneasy conversation, as a phase of all their lives
ends, a number of poetic texts are brought together.

> Because it is the day of Palms
> Carry a palm for me. . . .

Rocky then decides to inscribe some line on the window with
Helena's diamond ring, purportedly for the next inhabitants of
the room, but in fact with some desire to give a final expression
to his relationship with Mildred. He thinks of

> When my grave is broke up again
> Some second guest to entertain

and then decides on Dante's

> Nessun maggior dolore
> Che ricordarsi del tempo felice
> Nella miseria.

A page or two later, other quotations come to Mildred's mind:
'Lenten is come with love to town', and from *The Oxford Book of
English Verse* the thirteenth-century poem 'Deowes donketh the
dounes' (ch. 26). The movement in these quotations is backwards
in time, and downwards in mood, to a gloom as dense as the
alliterative medieval poem. Mildred has been disappointed.

Nevertheless, her life does not quite gather here, as the very
number of quotations, all approximate to her feelings, suggests.
Her friend the vicar Julian Mallory, who has become engaged
to a beautiful but unlikable clergyman's widow, Allegra Grey,
discovers her unkind intentions for his sister, and breaks off the

engagement: the sister, Winifred, is happy, and, by an osmosis, so is Mildred, who is also relieved of the entirely unjustified role of the disappointed rival which has been assumed for her by the parish. Furthermore, Helena's anthropologist friend, the severe Everard Bone, has begun to take an interest in Mildred: the novel ends with her sense of possibilities in both these areas of her life.

As in other Pym novels, the heroine narrowly escapes the fate of disillusioned hurt embitteredness. Three older women in the novel represent the various emotional possibilities for a woman. Everard Bone's mother is an eccentric, not wholly sane, cruel to her companion, narrowly religious, and obsesssed by macabre images of woodworm and of birds which drop their 'unpleasantness' or attack people: 'The Dominion of the Birds' (ch. 16). We do not know what accounts for this in Mrs Bone, but the imagery suggests repressed, disgusted, hostile relations in her psyche. The encroachment of such a possibility on Mildred is suggested by the discovery of extensive woodworm in the piece of Rocky's Victorian furniture she had admired. On the other hand there are the recurrent appearances of the splendid no-nonsense figure of Sister Blatt, one of the local parishioners. Sister Blatt is single woman gloriously herself and unaffected by men, and thus a tonic, as she snorts her laughter at the extreme delicacies of the local ladies or is glimpsed sailing by on her bicycle. At a depressed moment for Mildred, she even has words of advice: '"You're looking tired," she said suddenly. "Your face is quite grey. You must take care of yourself"' (ch. 23). When Allegra Grey moves out of the rectory, it is a friend of Sister Blatt's who moves in: '"Oh, no, my friend isn't at all the type to attract a man," said Sister Blatt with rough good humour. "There won't be any nonsense of that kind"' (ch. 25). Similarly, Rocky's and Helena's flat is taken over by a pair of equally splendid single women, with whom Mildred will have no difficulties sharing a bathroom. Afficionados of Italy, it is they who, discovering Rocky's inscription, recognise the misquotation, the addition of 'e' to 'maggior' to make 'maggiore': 'perhaps this person was thinking of Lago di Maggiore, no doubt it was the memory of a happy time spent there'. No doubt, for Rocky's facile romanticism has intruded even into his parting inscription, and this discovery provides a salutary reminder not only of the Wrens, but also of

Rocky's Italian mistress. The third older woman is the wife of the president of the anthropological society, glimpsed by Mildred dropping off to sleep over her knitting during the interminable lecture she attends: a reassuring figure of a woman comfortably herself while in relation to a man.

The novel reaches no concluding fulfilment, and even the completion of disillusionment has been balanced by the increasing possibilities elsewhere. At one point Mildred visits the office of a civil servant, brother of a friend. From his window, she can see across into the windows of another ministry:

> 'Ah, yes, the Ministry of Desire,' said William solemnly.
> I protested, laughing.
> 'They always look so far away, so not-of-this-world, those wonderful people,' he explained. 'But perhaps we seem like that to them. They may call *us* the Ministry of Desire.'   (ch. 8)

Perhaps over there desire is fulfilled. For the onlooker Mildred, who has looked on at Rocky's and Helena's marriage, there is an implied message, though Mildred, unlike Helena, has always been sensibly sceptical of *fulfilment* in either romance or career. The fulfilment of desire is always elsewhere, just as even the presentation of Mildred's own desire is displaced into the figures of Rocky's Wrens. In her own way, Pym provides an account of life that anticipates Derrida's 'concept' of *différance*, being at once always differed (differed from itself) and deferred. The view in this scene is through the window, the medium of desire, and Rocky's differed message, written for Mildred, was inscribed on a window pane. She has been the medium, the go-between of Rocky and Helena, so the inscription has a certain appropriateness. It suggests as well that the medium that is ourselves but not our presence or fulfilment, somewhere between first and third person, is the medium of writing. As will be argued in greater detail in Chapter 5, Pym's implied sense of language is by no means unsophisticated.

Jane and Prudence

Jane and Prudence was written between 1950 and 1952, and published in 1953. It is the only one of the novels for which there is no manuscript in the Bodleian, though some notebooks survive. Like *Excellent Women*, it sets lives lived around the church in relation to lives lived in London offices and institutions. Here the contrast is marked by placing the church life in a country parish so that the action of the novel follows the characters as they move up and down between country and city. Each locale has its heroine: Jane is the wife of a country vicar, Prudence the single working woman: the novel moves between their choices. The overall spirit of its examination is established by the introduction of the two principal characters, in the first chapter, at an Oxford women's college reunion. Prudence was Jane's student when Jane briefly tutored there: she is twenty-nine, Jane forty-one. There is enough difference between their ages for a degree of mutual incomprehension, but, as the reunion opening suggests, they both have to face the question, 'What have we women done?/What are we women doing these so many years later?' Some women have made splendid careers; many, like Jane, have married vicars; as for Prudence, 'She might have said, "and Prudence has her love affairs", thought Jane quickly', and perhaps this is what Prudence feels, though in the circumstances she cannot say so in so many words. What she does say is

> 'I don't need compensation. . . . I often think being married would be rather a nuisance. . . . I should hardly know what to do with a husband.'
> Oh, but a husband was someone to tell one's silly jokes to, to carry suitcases and do the tipping at hotels, thought Jane, with a rush. And though he did these things, Nicholas was a great deal more than that.   (ch. 1)

Prudence has the affairs, but Jane's rush of emotion shows her to be the romantic.

Prudence works at an undefined cultural organisation modelled on the African Institute. Its world, however, is presented in terms not of anthropology, but of the petty meannesses of office life. But, though anthropology is not named in connection with the office, it does run as undercurrent in the work, contributing richly to the comic effect. Pym's use of the sign system of food goes back to *Some Tame Gazelle*, and food and its consumption had a particular point in the post-war days of rationing, but it is also clear that anthropology gave her a new sense of deeper comic possibilities. As Jane's housekeeper explains,

> 'Father Lomax will have had his liver *last* time'. . . .
> 'Which won't be much consolation to him now,' said Jane, 'so he had better not see us eating it. Like meat offered to idols,' she went on.   (ch. 2)

Her family cannot see the idea, but Jane thinks that 'people in these days do rather tend to worship meat for its own sake' (ibid.) Particularly the idea of meat as idol worship connects with the female pursuit of men or tribute to men through the provision of meat. It is understood among the women characters of the parish that it is a part of the mysterious and even sexual nature of men ('They are different to us') that 'a man must have meat' (ch. 3). Pym makes an attractive comedy of a lunchtime in the village (ch. 5): Jane and her husband, Nicholas, the vicar, go out for lunch because Jane has neglected to supply even tins. They are guiltily pleased to be offered bacon and eggs, an item not on the menu. Jane finds she is served one egg, Nicholas two: 'a man needs eggs!' as the genteel lady proprietor explains. Shortly afterwards a regular male client is served chicken: 'Man needs bird', Jane reflects. The narrative then follows Fabian Driver, the village romantic lead, home to the dinner of grilled steak prepared by his housekeeper. There is a subtle sexual play in all this, of course, a recognition of what runs under the genteel surface. In addition, the imagery connects with allusions in the text to the conceits of seventeenth-century poetry: Fabian Driver will also eat a 'casserole of hearts' (ch. 3). Earlier we meet the parish ladies in the church decorating it with vegetables and flowers for the harvest festival, though one lady complains that 'Harvest service' has a less pagan sound: 'Harvest *Festival* has a rather different connotation, I feel.' That such connotations are not wholly inappropriate is shown by the arrival of Fabian Driver:

> 'What a fine marrow, Mr Driver,' said Miss Doggett in a bright tone. 'It is the biggest one we have had so far, isn't it Miss Morrow?' . . .

Jane felt that she was assisting at some primitive kind of
ritual at whose significance she hardly dared to guess.

(ch. 3)

The reader is sure that man needs meat to grow such a marrow.
Jane and Prudence is Barbara Pym's funniest novel, her most
humorous account of the romantic. For Prudence, for instance,
in love with her perfectly dreary elderly boss, 'the thought of
Arthur having to go without his elevenses was quite unbearable'
(ch. 4). Later, after receiving the tribute of a 'penetrating
look', she goes out for a drink with Fabian Driver, and the
novel's two beautiful people find that they do not have a lot to
say: 'their conversation did not improve very much even with
strong drink, though they gradually became more relaxed and
their eyes met so often in penetrating looks that it did not seem
to matter' (ch. 9). Or, the elderly Miss Doggett reflects on the
romantic career of Fabian:

'They say, though, that men only want *one thing* – that's the
truth of the matter.' Miss Doggett again looked puzzled; it
was as if she had heard that men only wanted one thing, but
had forgotten for the moment what it was.   (ch. 7)

The vain and feckless Driver is himself the frequent object of
this narrative comedy. His wife, Constance, has died and her
grave is adorned with his portrait. During her life, Fabian
conducted a succession of affairs, but since her death there has
been a change:

The shock of it all had upset him considerably, and although
there had been several women eager to console him, he had
abandoned all his former loves, fancying himself more in the
role of an inconsolable widower than as lover. Indeed, it was
now almost a year since he had thought of anybody but
himself.   (ch. 5)

This is perfectly turned.
Fabian is perfectly revealed and reduced during the course of
the novel, but he is not a significant-enough creature to be the
novel's focus. *Jane and Prudence* is more about women than about
men, and what it gives us is not, primarily, men's perception of

women, or even women's perception of men, but women's
perception of other women as they present themselves within
the field of romance.

The exchange of looks in married life offers little to attract
Prudence:

> 'So even my not drinking isn't an advantage,' said Jane. 'I
> might just as well take to it, then.' She poured herself a full
> glass of sherry.
>
> 'I shouldn't have it if you don't like it,' said Nicholas in an
> anxious tone. 'It seems a pity to waste it.'
>
> Jane flashed him a look which Prudence caught. She
> supposed that marriage must be full of moments like
> this. (ch. 8)

The cold of the house, the indifference to surroundings, the
sloppy perparation of food, the inattentiveness, all dismay
Prudence: 'Prudence remembered other houses where Jane and
Nicholas had lived and the peculiar kind of desolation they
seemed to create around them' (ibid.). In turn, visiting
Prudence's flat in London, with its neat Regency furniture,
Jane finds something too perfect about it, too much given to
appearance.

Jane is also distributed by Prudence's elaborate make-up:
'She found herself quite unable to look at Prudence, whose
eyelids were startlingly and embarrassingly green, glistening
with some greasy preparation which had little flecks of silver in
it' (ch. 9). This reaction proceeds her observation that Nicholas
is gazing at Prudence with admiration. Jane is initially affected
by Prudence's transparency, by a kind of nakedness that make-
up shows – not a paradox, because it is nakedness of intention.
At such moments, Jane feels a real distance from Prudence. All
Pru's apparatus, her over-elaborate dresses, her see-through
nightie, painted fingernails and toenails, and so on, are
estranged here because they are seen through a shocked female
eye, not the male eye for which they are intended. Pru's
awareness of this is shown in her small dread about Jane's
predictable hilarity at the name of an expensive perfume she
wears: such names expose dreams (ch. 8).

The novel's point of view is close to Jane's but it also shows
her, as a dowdy middle-aged woman, at moments of extreme

exposure to another woman's gaze. The point of view here is
that of Flora, Jane's self-possessed undergraduate daughter:

> Jane was sitting on the other side of the fire with her feet up
> on a pouffe . . . she had 'dropped off', as she frequently did
> on a Sunday afternoon, and her head was drooping over against
> the back of the chair; her mouth was slightly open too.   (ch. 6)

As Prudence's self-conscious appearance embarrasses Jane,
Jane's unself-consciousness embarrasses her daughter.

The argument, however, goes largely to Jane. Prudence is
irreligious and self-centred, though that is not the right word,
for she has more an image of herself than a self from which she
can relate. Her sentiments for her lovers are transient, and
there is something suggestive of Fabian Driver himself in her
little mental place of urns containing the ashes of their
memories. Her taste in reading is instructive if set against
Pym's resistance to certain modernisms: her bedtime novel
describes a love affair 'in the fullest sense of the word', though
in a 'very intellectual' way (ch. 4). Jane later characterises
such novels as being by Mr Green or Mr Greene: Henry Green
or Graham Greene (ch. 17). We compare Jane's own reaction
to modernism, which is shown in a most unsuitable comment at
a rather strained parish council meeting: 'I always think when
I am listening to some of these tense, gloomy plays on the
wireless, Ibsen and things like that, oh, if only somebody would
think of making a cup of tea!' (ch. 14).

Prudence has made the wrong choices, and her self is held in
an essentially defensive and brittle way, though it is not without
its satisfactions. Her relation to food is a sign of her choice.
Dining romantically with Fabian Driver she still has plenty of
thoughts for the smooth creamy sauce in which the chicken will
be served, and after her disappointment she treats herself to 'a
dry Martini and then a little smoked salmon', no more, until
the waiter suggests chicken:

> 'Well,' Prudence hesitated, 'perhaps just a slice of the
> breast. . . .' No sweet, of course, unless there was some fresh
> fruit, a really ripe yellow-fleshed peach, perhaps?   (ch. 20)

From attendance on a handsome man, Prudence has moved to
attendance on a handsome woman: a sort of fleshy narcissisism.

Pym allows Prudence a happy and hopeful ending, but what is most telling, after her disappointment with the clearly unsatisfactory Driver, is that she is obviously again going to make only a passing affair out of the relationship she has struck up with the young man at the office, Mr Manifold. Manifold is one of a series of men in Pym's fiction of a slightly lower class than her heroines. As we shall see, Pym's art is sometimes strained in her handling of such figures, but their inclusion is partially a recognition that some of what inhibits effective relations in her novels is class. Here the point is clearly made, for Manifold, despite his name (which is suggestive of the petit-bourgeois obsession with the motor car) is an attractive and interesting man. But Prudence, we feel, prefers her men 'in uniform,' as she prefers herself. When she is most unhappy she takes up and reads a volume of George Herbert given to her by Jane, where she finds

> I gave to Hope a watch of mine; but he
>   An anchor gave to me.
> Then an old Prayer-book I did present;
>   And he an optic sent.
> With that I gave a vial full of tears;
>   But he, a few green ears.
> Ah, loiterer! I'll no more, no more I'll bring;
>   I did expect a ring.

But Prudence cannot quite make the application. The narrative gives her hope, blesses here in a way, as her friendship with Jane has blessed her in ways she cannot appreciate, but she chooses for herself a different seventeenth-century poem, one more in accord with her self-defeating and facile modernism:

> Therefore the Love which us doth join
>   But Fate so enviously debars,
> Is the Conjunction of the Mind,
>   And Opposition of the Stars.

Pym remarks that Prudence seems 'satisfied with Marvell's summing-up of the situation' (ch. 23).

Jane is one of Pym's most lovable and amusing characters, a delightful centre of warmth and idiosyncrasy. She is early characterised by her 'outspokenness and her fantastic turn of mind', a kind of comic humour which is progressively deepened to suggest the mixed feelings about life of a wonderfully candid and generous nature. Her comic unself-consciousness, curiosity, romanticism, are developed at one point as we see her obscurely trying to approach some lost idea of herself:

> After supper Jane began rummaging in the drawer of her desk where her Oxford notebooks were kept, in which she recorded many of her thoughts about the poet Cleveland. . . . But when she began to read them she saw that the ink had faded to a dull brownish colour. . . . A line came into her head. *Not one of all of those ravenous hours, but thee devours.* . . . If only she were one of these busy, useful women, who were always knitting or sewing. Then perhaps it wouldn't matter about the ravenous hours. She sat for a long time among the faded ink of her notebooks, brooding, until Nicholas came in with their Ovaltine on a tray and it was time to go to bed. (ch. 13)

We have seen that Pym tends to characterise a career as a sort of futile egoistic triumph over time, and this again appears as a theme in *Less than Angels*. Thus it is clear that even useful women cannot escape the ravenous hours. It is clear too, by implication, that what led Jane to study her seventeenth-century poet was a sense of the truth of his matter that is opposed to academic ambition and the production of dissertations. It is time and time's work on the ideals of our youth that Jane grieves for, and for them there is no cure but Ovaltine and bed.

Similarly, for one's errors there is only acceptance. When Jane unintentionally offends at a parish meeting, her husband mildly tells her off. This reproof, which is made without bitterness or resentment, brings us to the heart of their relationship. It is, inevitably, a painful moment for Jane:

> She ran from the room and into the downstairs cloakroom where the sight of Nicholas's soap animals reminded her of her love for him and she might have wept had she not been past the age when one considers that weeping can do good or bring relief. (ch. 14)

And so she recovers herself, and the pair draw from Pym an untypical narrator's comment: 'And so they sat down on either side of the fire, two essentially good people', and Nicholas tells Jane his idea of growing his own tobacco (ibid.).

Jane's appreciation of Nicholas is considerable (she is, for instance, pleased that he has retained his figure), but his response to her is now perhaps as much contentedly benign and tolerant as anything else. The little soap animals that he buys himself (the occasion of a wonderfully comic scene in the novel) suggest a placid enjoyment of his life that falls short of the romantic. Time and this falling-away of Nicholas's romantic interest lead to Jane's interest in Pru's affairs, and, as she stands over the washing-up (which she does badly) in her untidy kitchen, she bursts out with 'Oh Prudence . . . you and Fabian must make a fine thing of your married life'. But Fabian is beginning to let Prudence down, and the depressing domestic scene becomes an image of her condition as well:

> Jane hadn't even any *long* spaghetti, she thought, the tears coming into her eyes . . . only horrid little broken-up bits. . . . When Jane and Nicholas came back from Evensong they found her crouching on the floor in the dining-room, delving in the dark sideboard cupboard among the empty biscuit barrels and tarnished cruets for the sherry decanter. (ch. 18)

What is good in Jane's life is suggested in a transformation of her kitchen. When the severely repressive Miss Doggett comes to inform Jane and Nicholas that she has suspicions that Fabian Driver and her companion are carrying on, she enters upon a scene of pleasant domestic confusion, Jane bottling her jam, Nicholas drying his tobacco:

> For not only was the table covered with all the paraphernalia of bottling – jars, metal caps, rubber rings, plums, jugs, kettles, and sheets of newspaper – but the kitchen itself seemed festooned with enormous green leaves which hung down from everywhere. . . . Miss Doggett held her hands up to her hat, feeling as if she were in some Amazonian jungle. (ch. 19)

Amongst this tropical vegetation is the benign vicar in a flowered apron. The scene brings together anthropological fertility, sexual equality and comic domesticity. It is a happy meeting of pagan and Christian, the jungle and the clear jars of fruit, of which Jane remarks, 'It seems to require such a very great deal of faith to lift them up by their glass tops' (ibid.). The clear glass, a glass of blessings, to be lifted by faith. It is from this scene that Jane marvellously marches out to confront Fabian on behalf of her injured friend, clad in the black clerical raincoat of her husband, which comes down to her ankles. Against such a figure of lovable and uninhibited selfhood, Prudence's image seems truly limited. What Jane has as a virtue of being herself is not romantic 'fulfilment', even attention, but a life. She and her husband share not romance, not some overwhelming meeting, but the interweaving of their fancies in an easy fond relation. If the mild and bespectacled Nicholas does not gaze at Jane any more, at least he does not demand of her an image. In Jane, Pym creates a woman free of the constraints of the male gaze, and, though there is a loss in that freedom, there is also the suggestion of some area of relationship more satisfying than the gaze allows.

Fabian Driver has, in fact, formed a relationship with Miss Doggett's companion, Jessica Morrow, or, rather, she has formed his essentially passive narcissism into a relationship. She will marry him, tired as he is of the effort of gazing and composing replies to Prudence's rather literary love letters. Jessica Morrow, who returns from *Crampton Hodnet* (see above, Chapter 2) is an interesting and unusual character amongst Pym's women. Though a professional companion to Miss Doggett, she is a woman who cannot be another woman's friend, for she is preoccupied by a private determination to get a man at any cost. In a novel very much about how women are seen, and how they see each other, she is an interesting case. What makes her effective with Fabian Driver is her total lack of illusion about either herself or him, and what makes her acceptable and even welcome to him is that her thorough knowledge of him, though expressed with a little asperity, has no effect on her desire. The narrative at times follows Jessica in the calculations which no one else can know, but, just before the confrontation with Miss Doggett and Jane, we are shown Miss Doggett examining her room, bare of all adornment, or personality. Jessica Morrow has chosen to live, or has been forced to live, an unillusioned life. Under Miss Doggett's eye

we see in her room the image of a life at once concealed and
revealed in its plain intentions, a self-possession which is a self-
denial. The incorporation of Jessica Morrow into the story
serves not just to round off nicely the story of Fabian Driver,
but also to suggest a way in which female desire can appear to
its own eyes, and what gazes it must meet. For Fabian, Jessica
dresses well just once, on the occasion when she risks forcing
him to commit himself. She wears a dress that was his dead
wife's, which she has sorted out as jumble, and is surprised that
he nearly recognises it, for beneath Fabian Driver's penetrating
glance there is a deep inattention.

Less than Angels: 'A Common interest in Africa'

Less than Angels was written in 1953–4 and published by Cape in
1955. The notes and drafts of the novel (MS Pym 16) reveal an
impressive clarity of conception and intention, particularly as
regards the use of the relations of the central male figure, Tom, to
a number of women as a structuring principle. *Less than Angels*,
Lord David Cecil wrote to Pym, after rereading it in 1979, 'I
like the best of all your books', but it is perhaps not at first the
most appealing of the novels, largely because Pym goes into
relatively unfamiliar territory. True, the heroine is in early
middle age, disappointed in love, and a romantic novelist, but
at thirty-one she is younger than other Pym heroines, and very
much the inhabitant of a world of flats, Greek restaurants and
wine parties, rather than of churches and fêtes. Many of the
other central characters are young postgraduates. Pym enters
into this postgraduate world with sufficient sympathy to make
Tom her most interesting male character; in no other novel,
until *Quartet in Autumn*, does she give so much from the male
point of view.

It is also a novel about the world of anthropology, though,
interestingly enough, what we see is characters moving away
from it, in different ways finding it insufficient. By contrast, the
church is hardly present in the novel, though the half-hearted
young anthropologist Deirdre can hear the bells of the nearby
church in her suburban bedroom, and, on the one occasion that
certain characters attend service, Pym remarks that 'there was
perhaps nobody who did not feel in some way the better' (ch.

7). This marginalising of the church is one sign of Pym's presentation of a crueller, harder world in this novel. Here the underlying poetic texts are not drawn from Victorian poetry, as in *Some Tame Gazelle*, or George Herbert, as in *A Glass of Blessings*. Victorian poets are the favourite reading of Catherine, but at a crisis in his commitment to anthropology Tom is puzzled when she quotes 'Dover Beach': he does not think that 'Victorian poets are much help these days' (ch. 9). But, as Catherine goes on to remark, Arnold's poem is not, in fact, 'a comfortable poem', and its modern sense of historical displacement is apt to his context in ways Tom cannot see. The reading of the characters in *Less than Angels* is largely in modern and tragic texts, Dostoevsky, Chekhov, and others; even the narrator characterises postgraduate life, only half humorously, by reference to Dostoevsky, and mentions a Henry Moore sculpture. Again, the title of the work is drawn not from the Romantics or the Victorians but from the harder satirical poetry of Pope. Above all, the world of anthropology is opened out in a constant interplay between African and European elements. This is partly comic, but it is also handled to suggest cruel and disturbing forces: if in *Some Tame Gazelle* Pym rejected T. S. Eliot and modernism, here it seems that the uses of anthropology in modernism are influential and may even be said to provide, or at least be analogous to, the essential poetic characterisation of the novel's world.

This 'anthropological' quality is apparent in the novel's opening as Catherine takes her tea in a London eating-house:

A confused impression of English tourists shuffling round a church in Ravenna, peering at mosaics, came to Catherine Oliphant. . . . These were large bright peacocks with speading tails, each one occupying a little alcove, almost like a side chapel in a cathedral. But why didn't the tray carriers make some obeisance as they passed the peacocks, or lay offerings of buns, poached eggs and salads on the ground before them? Catherine wondered. Obviously the cult of peacock worship, if it had ever existed, had fallen into disuse.

She poured herself another cup of tea. . . . She felt no guilt . . . for she earned her living writing stories and articles for women's magazines and had to draw her inspiration from everyday life, though life itself was sometimes too strong and

raw and must be made palatable by fancy, as tough meat
may be made tender by mincing.   (ch. 1)

The cultural displacement suggested by tourists is later
developed into a major theme. The idea of peacock worship,
though a typically wayward fancy of a Pym heroine, suggests
both the cult of female devotion to male egoism (Catherine and
Deirdre, her young rival for Tom's affections, later meet in the
same café) and a radiating if unperceived spiritual alternative.
Thus beneath the surface of comic incongruity runs the sense of
deeper, 'anthropological' significances. Similarly, Catherine's
fiction (like Pym's) may be 'mincing' in one sense, but the
image carries with it the anthropological suggestion of the
cultural importance of food preparation and the borders between
culture and nature. We later see Catherine

> mincing some cold meat in her mincing machine, which was
> called 'Beatrice', a strangely gentle and gracious name for
> the fierce little iron contraption whose strong teeth so
> ruthlessly pounded up meat and gristle. It always reminded
> Catherine of an African god with its square head and little
> short arms, and it was not at all unlike some of the crudely
> carved images with evil expressions and aggressively pointed
> breasts which Tom had brought back from Africa.   (ch. 2)

(The mincing-machine called 'Beatrice' appears in the notebooks
for *Some Tame Gazelle*.) Beatrice, like Ravenna, suggests an
Italianate, even Dantesque, religious code, but the main
suggestion here is the congruence of the heroine with ritual and
cultural forms of violence. As the romantic novelist, Pym has
also characterised her text as superficially euphemistic but
deeply powerful. The particular achievement of *Less than Angels*
does, in fact, lie in the co-operation of these two impressions, of
niceness, humour and Englishness, and something else.

It may be said that in *Less than Angels* Pym sets against
professional anthropology what might be called literary
anthropology, of a kind which she perhaps derived from Sir
James Frazer, whose *The Golden Bough* is praised in *Some Tame
Gazelle* for having literary qualities absent from the pseudo-
scientific prose of his successors in anthropology. Another
source may well have been T. S. Eliot, who was, of course,

himself influenced by *The Golden Bough*. When Alaric, the retired colonial administrator, is seen smiling through the suburban leaves, the reader may be reminded of early Eliot poems; at home, when alone, Alaric finds it easier if he wears one of his African masks. The lines from Elizabeth Barrett Browning that come unexpectedly into Catherine's mind at a moment of 'stress' and 'emotional upheaval' when Tom departs for Africa are in something like the Eliot vein:

> What was he doing, the Great God Pan,
> Down in the reeds by the river. . . .

The comic subplot of the novel tells of the promise of some much-sought-after research grants, flattered out of a wealthy American widow by the urbane Professor Mainwaring, and then not forthcoming, because the money is in turn wheedled away by one Father Gemini for his own projects. Mainwaring invites the prospective candidates down to his country home for a weekend of informal interviews, a comically self-indulgent gesture, but one which also suggests his need to express a self to his students other than the professional. Anthropology not only fails to deliver the grants, but the occasion allows Mainwaring, with a flamboyance that recalls the Archdeacon in *Some Tame Gazelle*, to pronounce on the limits of professional anthropology and to suggest the more fundamental meaning of what I am calling literary anthropology. The message of this is, like that of the lines from Pope that provide the novel's title, that man and his civilisation stand between angel and beast, between the spiritual and the other meaning of the peacock, between Beatrice and raw meat, and that his glory and humility lies in the recognition of this. The wall displays portraits of Mainwaring's ancestors:

> One was especially interesting and seemed to have some direct bearing on the art or science of anthropology. It was of a gentleman in eighteenth-century dress, attended by a turbaned Negro servant. The man held a skull in his hands and was gazing down at it thoughtfully. In the murky background two or three dim forms, men or even apes, could just be seen leaning against a ruined column. (ch. 18)

The scene in the picture, from the first great age of English empire, speaks of death and the beast, its sardonic perspective on the English world remains despite the cultured mediations of Mainwaring.

Anthropology enables Pym to introduce amusingly distanced remarks on English society – for instance, the comment of a young French student on the washing-up after Sunday dinner: 'I see; the older female relatives work in the kitchen when there are no servants' (ch. 7). Pym is also able to make comedy about the vague English ideas of Africa, derived partly from half-recollected hymns and like material:

> O'er heathen lands afar,
> Thick darkness broodeth yet. . . .
>   (in ch. 12)

But the comedy of anthropology can always give way to a darker vision, such as Catherine has after Tom's death:

> there are still lots of unpleasant diseases people can get, Tom used to tell me. A little worm that races about all over your body and the only time you catch it is when it goes careering across your eye-balls. . . .   (ch. 21)

The image suggests both madness and the grave, and, as effectively as anything in *Heart of Darkness*, it brings the African interior home.

Primarily, though, the professional study of anthropology is seen in this novel as the expression or consequence of a certain male egotistic separateness, the assumption of a petty authority over life and its relations. The central story is of Tom Mallow, ambitious young anthropologist, who progressively separates himself from a series of relationships. His course is charted in terms of sexual relations with three women – in chronological order, Elaine (the girl at home), Catherine and Deirdre. At the novel's beginning, Tom is in a relationship with Catherine, but he is already restless, seeking for a kind of female devotion to his work that he feels Catherine cannot provide; Catherine, we are later told, has too much personality in her own right. Tom, writing his thesis, wishes to be taken seriously, as an authority. Meeting the young and ready-to-be-devoted Deirdre, he begins to move away from Catherine. What is attractive about the scenes that show the end of their relationship is not only the clear candour with which Catherine experiences her pain, but also the way in which it is shown that Tom still boyishly depends on her to help him even as he is leaving her for another woman:

> 'Catty, please, I don't want to go *now.*' Tom suddenly realised that he was very tired. . . . He hadn't really meant to start anything; perhaps in the morning they would realise that it had all been a mistake.   (ch. 9)

Tom is not going to move in with Deirdre, only to a dreary post graduate flat, though there he will be freer to pursue his relationship with her. But the pursuit is half-hearted. What he seeks is not discoverable with her, and in the central scene between them, a walk in a suburban park, Pym finely communicates the degree to which he is lost. The relation of his thoughts to his romantic responses is nicely caught:

> 'Yes, your mother will want to see you,' said Deirdre dutifully.
> 'I suppose she will, but she isn't the kind of person who shows her feelings, and my brother is there all the time.'
> 'Which can't be quite the same,' said Deirdre warmly.
> . . . Two figures, followed at some distance by an old fat sealyham, came towards them. They seemed to be talking about the Test Match. Tom suddenly wished he were walking with them, making manly conversation, away from the cloying sweetness of love or, better still, at home with his typewriter, working on his thesis. For the end was in sight and it was going to be finished after all. He gave Deirdre's arm a sudden joyful squeeze and quickened pace.   (ch. 12)

The connections between Tom's feelings for his mother, his pursuit and evasion of relationships with women, and his desire for the masterful alienation of anthropology are clear here. A certain wistfulness is opened up, even in his callowness, as though he were reluctantly moving into loneliness. The course of his life, which seems to be the consequence of a deeper need and fear, serves only to isolate him. His past with his first, girl-

next-door love, Elaine, is shown to be irretrievably distant. He
is left with a sense of regret for the person he was and the life he
was once part of: 'He found himself mourning the young man
of those days, who went for long country walks and quoted
poetry.' On his return to London, Catherine rubs salt into the
wound:

> 'Your people wait for you,' said Catherine. 'How soothing it
> will be to get away from all this complexity of personal
> relationships to the simplicity of a primitive tribe . . .
> which you can observe with the anthropologist's calm
> detachment.'   (ch. 16)

Anthropology becomes a metaphor of a male need to make
relationship on the basis of separateness, assured identity and
knowledge. But Catherine's words 'Your people wait for you',
which refer to Tom's tribe, are cruel, for his people, at home
and in London, seem more easily to accept his successive
choices of self-distancing than he himself does. Tom has become
a tribeless wanderer, and it is not wholly surprising, though it
is shocking in its arbitrariness, when he is accidentally killed in
an African riot, in which he becomes involved, more out of
curiosity than out of passionate conviction' (ch. 20).

Thus, though the novel shows Tom successively disappoint a
series of women, it is he who seems in the end most pathetic
and excluded. The women grieve, but their emotional candour
enables them to accept loss and to resume relations with others.
Earlier, when Tom abandons Catherine, her natural emotional
and imaginative responsiveness lead her, after the first shock,
quickly to take an interest in the retired colonial administrator
and amateur anthropologist Alaric Lydgate. Alaric's relation to
anthropology is instructive. He is a bitter reviewer who cannot
write up his own notes. To Catherine, Alaric has the appearance
of an Easter Island statue, but the African masks he wears at
home only indicate his inability to accept and live in terms of a
vulnerable affective self. His relationship with Catherine is
rather sketchily presented, but Pym's idea is clear when she has
Catherine persuade him that he would be a relieved man if he
could burn his books. To the horror of his fellow anthropologists,
that is what he does, dancing at night around a suburban
bonfire with Catherine, the two of them wearing his African

masks. It is at the end of this chapter (ch. 20) that the narrator reports that Tom has died. The completeness of his alienation at the moment of his death is metaphorically expressed by his *whiteness*, in contrast not only to the Africans among whom he dies, but also to the masked Alaric and Catherine in the scene she has initiated.

The chapter that follows this news (ch. 21) brings together and develops the complex and fierce ironies of this work. For those at home and alive in England, Tom's death has an ambiguous value, if any, and its scene is largely filtered through the stereotypes of the English perceptions of Africa. There is something horrible from which the characters must turn, and even something absurdly pretentious about his death. Grief creates a community from which he was already self-excluded: Catherine now stays with Deirdre's pleasant family in the suburbs; Deirdre, in turn, finds support in another young anthropologist, Digby, whose wife she will become. Towards the chapter's end, Catherine looks out of her window and contemplates the prospect of Alaric with, as it were, her knowledge of Tom:

> Catherine got out of bed and stood by the window for some time, looking into the darkness of Alaric Lydgate's garden. Was there some movement there – did a masked figure on stilts move swiftly along the hedge – was that the low hum of a bull-roarer or only the wind in the apple trees? . . . she felt somehow responsible for him since the evening when they had burned his notes. Like so many men, he needed a woman stronger than himself, for behind the harsh cragginess of the Easter Island façade cowered the small boy, uncertain of himself. (ch. 21)

Catherine, the delightfully charming and loving romantic novelist, here looks out with an eye of knowledge more powerful and penetrating than that of the anthropologist, and looks *at the anthropologist*, seeing in him the congruence with the primitive male fending off his fear of the dark and female strength. It is such knowledge, rather than willingness to affection and relation, which seems dominant at the end of *Less than Angels*. The concluding chapter of the novel repeats this motif, establishing it in the world of nice English women. The last

ritual gathering of Tom's women is at a women's club in
London, as though they were now among the imperialists
('Catherine . . . was not clear as to the function of the club. . . .
It must, she thought, be something to do with Empire or
politics'): here they dispose of Tom's writings and of his
collection of African carvings (' "Oh, some of them are positively
rude!" said Catherine'). Then there is a last view from the
window of the Swan's, in which this time Catherine herself
appears:

> 'All the masks out on the lawn,' she said, 'and now – oh, my
> goodness – he's got a great big shield and two spears and
> some moth-eaten old feather thing. . . . Catherine is helping
> him – what *can* they be doing? Why now she's standing up
> and her arms are full of rhubarb! . . . What odd turns life
> does take!' And how much more comfortable it sometimes
> was to observe it from a distance, to look down from an
> upper window, as it were, as the anthropologists did.
>
> (ch. 23)

But this woman's view is combined with a woman's involvement:
knowledge and relation, within which the English scene –
bonfires, gardens, rhubarb – attains its own 'anthropological'
richness.

A Glass of Blessings

A Glass of Blessings was written in 1955–6 and published by
Cape in 1958: it is the last of the four comedies of these
intensely creative years (1949–56). The notebook for *A Glass of
Blessings* (MS Pym 17) is particularly interesting, recording
Pym's gradual arrival at her delightful heroine and her world.
The notebook opens with an early title for the novel: 'THE LIME
TREE BOWER', from Coleridge's 'The Lime Tree Bower My
Prison', though it is not clear at what stage Pym introduced it.
The first note establishes the idea of a 'Vicar of a fashionable or
city church – very high the kind of vicar who could be
telephoned to luncheon, and I(?) hear the bell trilling in the
middle of the service (lunchtime)' (fo. 1). The novel's superb
opening is immediately established (see Introduction), and the

next note introduces the idea of a friend whose brother has lost his job through 'drink and scandal' and to whom the heroine is attracted.

But the character of the narrator–heroine is undecided. Pym speculates on her being an office worker, or perhaps 'a widow' with 'a house with "rather nice things". Something of a church crawler' (fo. 1). Two pages later, the first draft of the opening is preceded by the heading 'Characters' and the note 'the narrator – a widow or perhaps even divorced rejected (or has this been overdone?) 39 years old, has lost her husband in the war and now grown used to her state – but quotes Donne . . . these rags of heart . . .'(fo. 3). The delightfully elegant and naïve Wilmet has not yet appeared: the idea is still relatively satirical, the heroine more a Leonora (*The Sweet Dove Died*) than a young woman in whom beautiful feelings can grow. It is interesting, however, that a few lines below, in the draft opening, the heroine's age is corrected from thirty-nine to thirty-three.

Then, two pages later, there is a most interesting note, headed 'Oswestry – lovely hot weekend. July 9th–10th'. This heading makes it clear that Pym was now about to bring her heroine closer to her own feelings. The narrator introduces the scene with 'I go to stay with a woman friend, perhaps now liberated from her mother.' But the scene that is described provides the essentials of the visit Wilmet makes to a place of retreat late in *A Glass of Blessings*. It is a green and private place, with deckchairs for lazing in the sun, and lines from Marvell's 'To his Coy Mistress',

My vegetable love should grow
Vaster than Empires and more slow

are quoted. Pym then notes, 'Birds are tame and cheeky – larger than life – Blackbirds and thrushes come bumping and swooping – then says seem louder and more aggressive' (fo. 5). With these notes Pym had arrived at the novel's poetic centre and its point of resolution. By associating Wilmet with her own feelings of sensuous openness, she added to her character's social façade a potential for real feeling.

It therefore became necessary to recast Wilmet's circumstances and the events of the novel. In the notes that follow, Piers is at first still a heterosexual; the husband, Noddy, who is now introduced, has a 'fundamental coldness' of nature (fo. 9v). These details suggest that neither the comedy nor the optimism of the novel as we have it has been quite grasped. A key moment in this shift would seem to be the establishment of Sybil, Wilmet's mother-in-law, as a powerful and interesting figure in drafts for chapters 2 and 3. After these drafts, another list of 'characters' (accompanied by the amusing note '"Oh, I like a crowded canvas!" says BP') is made in which the characters are all more or less as they appear in the novel and in which the comic plot of Wilmet's self-deception is implied: Piers has a 'friend, who shares his flat', called Squirrel, or Keith or Raymond; Rowena, Wilmet's friend, has a 'flirty husband' (fo. 34v). In the misplaced feeling for Piers, and the confusion occasioned by Harry, Rowena's husband, Wilmet's well-meaning willingness is carried through as the essential movement of feeling in the novel. The establishment of Sybil has ensured that it will be protected. The notebook thus shows Pym moving from a somewhat satirical approach to her heroine to a more delighted comic conception: the turning-point would appear to be that sunny weekend at Oswestry.

A Glass of Blessings as we have it is the most charming, accomplished and purely delightful of Pym's novels. It may be described as Barbara Pym's *Emma*, a superbly designed comedy of an attractive and lively heroine's misapprehension of her situation and the feelings of those around her. Wilmet is married to Rodney, a senior civil servant. She is young, attractive, elegantly dressed and idle. She is also, we gradually perceive, deeply ingenuous. Bored with her life, though she does not put it to herself like that, Wilmet develops a romantic interest in the amusingly named Piers Longridge, the brother of her best friend. Piers is restless, between lovers, and perhaps insecure in his homosexuality. He allows Wilmet to become interested in him, finding her attractive company. A mysterious Christmas gift to Wilmet, leads her to believe that he is interested in her, though it turns out that the gift is the expression of the middle-aged restlessness of her friend's husband, Harry. All the same, Piers seems particularly happy the next time he meets her. Wilmet, though, is to be disillusioned: Piers is happy because he has met a young man. The plain but good church-going woman Mary, who has made a reluctant friend of Wilmet, marries a handsome priest. Rodney, Wilmet's apparently dull husband, has himself been on the verge of an affair with an attractive woman friend of a female colleague. Things were not at all as Wilmet thought they were. These events take place between one summer and the next: a winter's tale with a summer's end.

A bald summary of events is less than usually adequate here, however. The achievement of *A Glass of Blessings* depends primarily on the medium of its telling, which is to say on the adoption of Wilmet as narrator. The art is to tell a story that depends on a succession of discoveries, the likelihood of which is not apparent to the narrator until the events occur, and the full significance of which may not even then be understood by her. The deeper achievement is that this mode of telling becomes a subtle elaboration of Wilmet's mode of presenting herself to the world and to herself.

Wilmet is in a way self-conscious: 'I thought we must have made quite a pleasing picture – two tall tweedy young Englishwomen embracing on a Surrey roadside' (ch. 3). But her self-consciousness is very unself-conscious in another way: 'I was pleased at his compliment for I always take trouble with my clothes, and being tall and dark I usually manage to achieve some kind of distinction' (ch. 1). This vanity, if that is what it is, is touching and seeks reassurance. Wilmet is not quite aware enough of herself to not be engaging and a little ridiculous: '*Vogue* or *Harper's* had urged us to "make it a lavender spring this year" and I had responded with too much haste and enthusiasm' (ch. 2).

This concern for her appearance is not just a minor detail, for Wilmet always seems to present herself to herself and hence to the reader *nicely dressed*. Wilmet observes her world, sometimes with touches of asperity, but she seeks to avoid presenting an attitude other than that of cultivated niceness. She reflects, but she keeps her reflections at a comic distance from her feelings and her situations. Even at the novel's end, she is unrevealing. When she and Rodney have confessed and laughed at their near infidelities,

I began to think that perhaps it wasn't so funny after all. I had always regarded Rodney as the kind of man who would never look at another woman. The fact that he could – and had indeed done so – ought to teach me something about myself, even if I was not yet quite sure what it was.

(ch. 22)

Wilmet never returns to this reflection. The novel remains a masterpiece of understatement. Nothing is explained, or tied up, as in a detective story. Wilmet is too well bred to interrogate experience, perhaps too fragile. Typically, Pym marks off her technique here by a comparison with modernist practice. Giving blood, Wilmet encounters an old lady (like a character ahead of time from *Quartet in Autumn*) who is obsessed by the fact that the blood she has come to donate is Rhesus negative, which the Regional Director has described in a letter as 'This precious blood'.

'This precious blood,' she murmured, and began muttering to herself. . . . It seemed like a 'stream of consciousness' novel. . . . Virginia Woolf might have brought something away from the experience, I thought; perhaps writers always do this, from situations that merely shock and embarrass ordinary people.   (ch. 6)

As a writer, though, Pym is close to the 'ordinary people'. Wilmet's choice of a presentableness, even in her self-presentation, is a kind of fineness, such as she does rightly detect in herself and her friend. It is this that makes us believe in her essential innocence and rightness, and which hence makes her so lovable. It is a sort of standard she will always meet, we feel.

Wilmet's openness and even inconsequentiality also make her a clear glass to her experience as she does attend to it. The opening of the novel, in its immediacy and thematic significance, is one of Pym's finest:

I suppose it must have been the shock of hearing the telephone ring, apparently in the church, that made me turn my head and see Piers Longridge in one of the side aisles behind me. . . . I found myself wondering where it could be and whether anyone would answer it.   (ch. 1)

Later her experience or romantic joy at Piers's apparent attentions and interest is candidly unfeigned. And it is this

vulnerability that constitutes the interest of the novel. Wilmet
might 'fall' in two ways as the action progresses: into an affair
that she would regret, that would destroy her deeper security
(which is nicely communicated through the repeated scenes at
the home of her mother-in-law, where she and her husband
live), and muddy her image of herself; and, then, as the novel's
revelations proceed (particularly that Piers is gay) there is
temptation to make of disappointment and the sense of folly a
kind of despair, cynicism or self-hatred. What protects her
immediately from the jar of having gone to Piers with her arms
open only to find him in the arms of a bland young gay, Keith,
is a feeling almost of maternity for Keith's gauche ways. But
disappointment grows on her: she falls into 'belittling' herself,
as Mary tells her, to whom she remarks that 'Life isn't always
all it's cracked up to be'. She feels she has discovered that she is
'in fact rather a horrid person' and these are not feelings that
she can communicate easily either to herself or to others (ch.
18). The danger of Wilmet's self-presentation is that she has
difficulty making some things acceptable to herself. Keith's
gaucheness forces something to the surface:

> 'Did you know what he said?' I asked.
> 'Did I know?' Keith seemed surprised. 'But of course. Piers
> really doesn't really think you're unlovable, you know, and *I*
> certainly don't.   (ch. 19)

This is not all that Wilmet wants to hear, and it is not sensitive
of Keith to say it, but the emotional candour he assumes, cheap
though it is, is helpful to Wilmet, whose ability to share her
feelings with her woman friends has passed with their marriages,
and who has little or no idea of what men are like.

But Wilmet is not safe until she briefly joins Mary on a
religious retreat. *A Glass of Blessings* is among Pym's more
churchy novels, though the 'tea' element, as Wilmet puts it, is
amply compensated for by the nice evocation of well-to-do life
in the world, the 'Martini' element. Wilmet is church-going,
but she is never quite the friend to Mary that Mary's ready-
heartedness would make her, and we perceive with Wilmet
something emotionally clichéd in Mary's career as first devoted
but downtrodden companion to aged mother, then would-be
bride of Christ, and shortly thereafter bride to the handsome

would-have-been celibate Father Ransome. Mary is good, but
Wilmet is finer, and the novel does not ask us to make a choice
that its own appreciations would make difficult. All the same,
the retreat is for Wilmet the return to happiness, though,
characteristically, the processes are indirect. In the novel's first
summer weather Wilmet saunters into a Marvellian green
world:

> Here, in a kind of greenish twilight, stood a pile of grass
> cuttings and garden rubbish, and as I added my pods to it I
> imagined all this richness decaying in the earth and new life
> springing out of it. Marvell's lines went jingling through my
> head.

> My vegetable love should grow
> Vaster than Empires and more slow . . .

> There seemed to be a pagan air about this part of the garden, as
> if Pan – I imagine him with Keith's face – might at any moment
> come peering through the leaves. The birds were tame and
> cheeky, and seemed larger than usual; they came bumping and
> swooping down, peering at me with their bright insolent eyes,
> their chirpings louder and more piercing than I had ever heard
> them.   (ch. 20)

A Glass of Blessings is sparing of literary allusion for one of
Pym's novels. This is both a sign of her ability to vary her narrative
mode, and appropriate to Wilmet's inexplicit relation to her
own feeling (an exception is her evocation of Eliot's *The Waste
Land* at the beginning of chapter 13). We only gather that she
has favourite poetry when Mary annoys her by quoting the
lines beginning 'There is a wind where the rose was' in reference
to her own feelings (ch. 6). Typically, too, it is Mary, at her
wedding, who provides the lines from George Herbert which
are the novel's title and epigraph, though by then Wilmet is
willing to take the quotation in her own way. This garden
passage, then, with its wonderful suggestions of a number of
Marvell poems, of metaphysical conceit, and the naturalism of
medieval painting, marks a restoration, or perhaps initiation,
for Wilmet into a positive relation to her own feelings, an

acceptance of them. The imagery is carried further when the bees swarm and an elderly priest comes out to smoke them:

> 'They must find the queen, that is the thing,' said one of the priests, 'then they will follow her to the hive.'
> I saw him take out a little note book and jot something down. It pleased me to think that here in this pagan part of the garden he might have found an idea for a sermon.
>
> (ch. 20)

Wilmet has found her queen, it may be said, though the reader need not follow the priest into drawing an explicit moral from the garden.

This summer scene and the growth of Wilmet's feelings have been nicely prepared for by an imagery of Italy and holidays that runs through the novel. During the war, Wilmet and Rowena, like Pym herself, were stationed where they knew the Rocky Napier of *Excellent Women* (other characters from *Excellent Women* and from other novels are mentioned with less point) and met their husbands: Rowena's Harry, for instance, is now grey-haired and more pompous than 'in the days when I had stood on his shoulders to write my name on the ceiling of an officers' mess somewhere near Naples'. Part of the attraction of Rodney for Wilmet at that time was that he seemed like a piece of home, with all its securities.

The Italian imagery runs through the work. For example, Wilmet's most romantic time with Piers is a walk by the riverside on which they come across a warehouse, a lumber room of memories, that takes on a Turneresque, Venetian aspect. However, the idea of keeping an Italian dream is gradually criticised as it reveals itself, practically, as only a taste for Italian restaurants, wines and 'decors', such as would be to Keith's taste. After Wilmet's disillusionment over Piers, her memories of her time in Italy with Rodney become fragmented, but the suggestion is that in parting from them she is moving into a new and more vital phase of her life:

> I tried to remember our time in Italy, but all that came into my mind were curious irrelevant little pictures – a dish of tangerines with the leaves still on them; the immovable shape of Rodney's driver as we held hands in the back of some

strange army vehicle on our way home from a dance; the dark secret face of a Neopolitan boy who used to come to stoke the fire in winter; then Keith's face peering through the leaves. . . . (ch. 20)

The choice is not as simple as between the two titles for clerical novels that Wilmet and Rodney invent: *Remembering Scampi* and *Cod on Fridays* (ch. 22). Thus, though Wilmet and Rodney take their holidays not in Portugal, as Wilmet had planned, but in rainy Cornwall, they there come across a room decorated with Neopolitan scenes, renewed memories which lead Rodney to his confession and, in turn, to renewed intimacy.

Thus *A Glass of Blessings* is a comedy in the deeper sense that goes beyond textual wit. It is about the restoration of romance, life, joy. Wilmet's experiences are so clearly and candidly and ingenuously presented in the glass of her self-presentation that the significance of the events seems to deepen in the reader, as it does in her, like a feeling – a gathering joy – rather rather an argument or insight. The title, a phrase from George Herbert's 'The Pulley', perfectly catches this effect of a still, bright, lucid welling-up of joy and happiness, the sense of being blessed by life: 'there was no reason why my own life should not be a glass of blessings too. Perhaps it always had been without my realizing it' (ch. 23). Great comedy – Shakespeare's, Dickens's – can give this impression of an unfathomable felicity, one of art's finest gifts.

In this respect, one of the most attractive things about *A Glass of Blessings* is that Wilmet probably never realises the whole of what has transpired to bring about her felicity. As with Jane Austen's *Emma*, where the reader may only very much later realise who bought Jane Fairfax a piano and when, Pym leaves us to gather it all. Wilfred Bason had to leave the Civil Service because he appropriated a little jade ornament, as he later appropriates Father Thames's Fabergé egg: the reader may never realise that it was through this incident that Rodney met his flirtation, Prudence Bates. More significantly, Wilmet is never seen to perceive, and perhaps the reader does not fully perceive, how much she and her marital situation have been read by her mother-in-law, Sybil. Wilmet admires Sybil's 'bleakly courageous agnosticism' (ch. 1), though she does not share it. She does not realise that Sybil is aware that Rodney is straying, and that Rodney is uncomfortably aware that she is aware. This mutual knowledge, to which Wilmet is not part, comes to a head at one of the family dinners:

> 'Yes. I see now that is the clue to Piers' lack of success in this world. I believe that he has loved not wisely but too well.'
> 'Mother, that's such a hackneyed quotation, and it really tells one nothing. I suppose we've all done that in our time, if you come to think of it.'
> I looked at Rodney in surprise. He so seldom indulged in these generalizations about love. I saw that he had gone a little pink.
> 'Noddy, I think you misunderstand me,' said Sybil.
>
> (ch. 19)

Having forced this confession out of Rodney, Sybil can let him off. But she does more than this. She marries the nicely agnostic-sounding Professor Arnold Root, forcing Wilmet and Rodney to holiday alone together, and turns them out of her house, which further forces them upon each other. After that news, Wilmet innocently remarks that 'I've always seen her as being rather like a character in Greek tragedy, doing some unnatural thing' (ch. 19). In *Less than Angels*, Catherine Oliphant had thought of life 'as an old friend, or perhaps tiresome elderly relative, pushing, knocking, clinging, but never leaving her alone, having the power to grant her moments of happiness but being very stingy with them just now' (ch. 13). Sybil is an elderly relative, but in her clear though apparently bleak charity she brings about a happier destiny for her son and daughter-in-law. If Pym's novels can be seen as repeatedly enacting a return to the parental home and the role of the mother, then here the mother forces the heroine out into life.

4

Transition

In his Foreword to *An Unsuitable Attachment* Philip Larkin divided Pym's novels into two groups: the high-spirited comedies written before the rejection of *An Unsuitable Attachment*, and the subsequent more sombre novels. Larkin had a tale to tell: of a happy author driven into gloom by the insensitivity of publishers and the inane literary standards of the swinging sixties. No doubt the rejection of *An Unsuitable Attachment* had its effect, but Pym's artistry was changing well before that event. After the four poised comedies of the period 1949–56, there is a perceivable slackening of invention and a less certain hold on the artistry, accompanied by uneasy attempts at new effects. This change is reflected in the increased length of composition time: three years (1957–60) for *No Fond Return of Love*, five years (1960–5) for *An Unsuitable Attachment*, six years (1963–9) for *A Sweet Dove Died*. It is also apparent in the strained and sketchy quality of much of *No Fond Return of Love*, its lack of poetic texture, general air of indirection, heavy recourse to characters from the earlier fiction, and authorial self-consciousness, which together make it the least satisfactory of the novels published in Pym's lifetime. The rejected novel, *An Unsuitable Attachment*, is denser and more poetic in its texture, and more ambitious in its theme, but the hold on the material is uncertain, particularly in regard to the central relationship, and there also Pym resorted at a slack moment to the introduction of characters from earlier novels. It is not wholly surprising that the Cape readers were not convinced by *An Unsuitable Attachment*; its rejection, however crassly managed and, with hindsight, myopic, is not attributable solely to the climate of the fiction of the day. *The Sweet Dove Died* is, as we have it, a finely formed work, but the struggle to arrive at this result was a long one and was importantly affected by an intervention by Larkin. However, with the book's successful completion, Pym arrived at a new stage in her writing.

No Fond Return of Love

Indeed, it can be said that, rather than simply suffering from the literary climate of the 1960s, Pym was herself in *No Fond Return of Love* uneasily experimenting with the self-conscious and self-referring fiction of the period. In her work this seems a blemish, but this experimentation reveals in a crude and unsatisfactory way something that is otherwise a very important characteristic of her fiction. In other words, Barbara Pym's work did not need such developments because their essentials were already part of her art.

There are three books of notes and drafts for *No Fond Return of Love* (MS Pym 18/1–3). At the beginning of the notes, Pym seeks to establish two women characters, Viola, christened Violet, and Dulcie (it takes a few experiments to establish this name). She asks herself, 'What is their relationship? How do they come to live together?' She then sketches a scene on a holiday in France in which the two women's personalities rub each other the wrong way. This idea is quickly replaced by the idea of bringing them together at a conference and then having Viola evicted from her flat so she moves in with Dulcie. Pym's first conception, then, was to establish two women together who did not have a great deal in common. The question then arose as to what to do with them. She speculated whether 'Dulcie is engaged in some kind of quest . . .' or research, and then: 'It could start off like this but in the course of it she falls in love with a young man half her age.' Then, on a loose sheet inserted in her little exercise book, she thought of Aylwin Forbes and the developed idea of Dulcie's quest. The elements of the novel now came together rapidly:

I. ⎫
II. ⎬ At the conference – Dulcie, Viola and Aylwin Forbes
III.   Dulcie at home. Her neighbours. Meeting Viola again.

It is about a woman who becomes interested in a man at a learned conference. She finds out more and more about him until at last his relations become more interesting to her than he is, and he eventually fades out of the picture altogether.

Then we don't want the young girl in at all – It would be better if Dulcie lived with her awkward relations? Or if they come to live with her? Though she might have a sister
Aylwin might well fall for the young girl, though
    Viola is desperate to get married – perhaps in the end she might get Dulcie's Clive – his pleading look. Could have a scene with them discussing past love.

It would be better if Dulcie's Uncle and Aunt lived somewhere nearer to Aylwin, as well as to his brother's parish.

Viola, perhaps, hasn't known AF well – but on seeing her in the gardens in her red canvas shoes he remembers her as 'that rather embarrassingly intense woman' who had wanted to talk about his work.

Dulcie has perhaps suffered her disappointment more recently than 6 years ago – or is younger than 35?

Perhaps the clergyman is AF's *cousin*. His brother and mother run the hotel. Something disgraceful about the brother. Or 'an interesting family' – all different.   (fo. 5)

This is a fine page of notes in which Pym's quick development of the ramifications and possibilities of an idea can be seen. It does not, however, describe the novel as we have it, because in that Aylwin Forbes does not fade out of the picture. Three stages in the process of imagining *No Fond Return of Love* can thus be discerned: in the first, two women characters are established together; in the second, that relationship is subordinated to the interest in a male, though the idea is still that a larger interest than the male should prevail; in the third, the interest in the male is what prevails. The movement is thus towards romantic fantasising on behalf of Dulcie.

In one perspective, the story of *No Fond Return of Love* is the story of the progress through a series of women's affections of a good-looking middle-aged academic, Aylwin Forbes. Not a great deal is given from his point of view (nothing to compare with Tom in *Less than Angels*, for instance), and the interest is rather in the emotions and relations of the women, who are, in a measure, brought together through him. Pym had previously worked such an assemblage of characters very successfully, but

here does less well. To begin with, Aylwin Forbes is too
emotionally limited to be an interesting object, and this raises a
question about the attention paid him by the female characters,
notably Dulcie. We are told that Aylwin has an almost Greek
beauty – 'Like a Greek marble, or something dug up in the
garden of an Italian villa, the features a little blunted, with the
charm of being not quite perfect' (ch. 2) – but he is shown to
have little character. Rocky Napier in *Excellent Women* has a
genuine if unsatisfactory charm which makes him a great comic
creation; Tom, in *Less than Angels*, has an obscure self-defeated
sadness in his selfishness which is even more interesting. But
Aylwin is just a pretty face. Looking up his entry in *Who's Who*
and finding that he has listed his interests as 'Conversation and
wine', Dulcie feels a slight distaste, as well she might, but this
does not inhibit her romantic interest. It is hard, Dulcie reflects
at one point, to explain Aylwin's rareness; to the reader it is
never explained, and his passage through a series of shallow
emotional responses trivialises him and the women who continue
to find him interesting.

In addition, the interrelations between the women are not
well developed. One of the interests of *Jane and Prudence* was
women's observations of each other's lives; in *Less than Angels*
the relations between women linked by one man are the source
of interesting and even painful comedy. There are interesting
moments between the women in *No Fond Return of Love*, but the
movement is always away from relationship. Dulcie's horror at
Viola's and Laurel's untidiness rapidly leads to a final decision
for separateness:

> 'There's plenty of milk in the larder,' said Dulcie,
> reassuming, much to Laurel's relief, her normal aunt-like
> manner. 'Take it from the bottle that's already started.
> Would you like to have coffee with me this evening?' she said
> to Viola. 'I don't suppose you'll want to get started on the
> index tonight, will you?'
> It was nice to think that Laurel was really using that gas-
> ring, making herself coffee. Soon the three of them would all
> be making their little separate drinks.   (ch. 8)

The separate little drinks seem to suggest that some women can
only comfort themselves, and not each other, when there is no
man in their lives.

This points to the problem of presentation in *No Fond Return
of Love*. Pym's female characters normally have their romantic
desires and their friendships. Here there is less than usual of
friendship. Similarly, the novels normally set up a little
interrelated world of characters the experience of all of whom is
registered, and *No Fond Return of Love* is unusually unsuccessful
in this respect. Minor comic characters such as Dulcie's
neighbour, Senhor Macbride Pereira, or Mrs Beltane, are
presented in very limiting terms. No interest is developed in
Dulcie's Uncle Bertram and Aunt Hermione: indeed, like Mrs
Beltane, they seem to call up only a kind of narrative asperity
and distaste. An entire subplot, concerning Aylwin's brother,
the priest Neville, and one of his female parishioners, goes
undeveloped.

The novel is less of an imagined world than the working-out
of a fantasy for the Pym character, Dulcie, in whose interests all
other elements are sacrificed. Neville is included only to add a
possible extra area of interest to Dulcie's future life (she might
live in his parish one day). More importantly, the other female
characters are sacrificed to Dulcie. Viola is the typical foil to
the Pym heroine, demanding and unwittingly selfish. Dulcie is
early struck by her make-up – 'the sallow face certainly looked
bizarre and striking' (ch. 1) – and the novel she toys with
writing is of predictable type:

> 'I'm sure,' she added hastily, 'that yours will be awfully
> good. I should think you have the gift for observing people
> and getting them down on paper.'
> 'Oh, it won't be *that* kind of novel,' said Viola
> distastefully. (ch. 4)

But Viola is not sufficiently presented in her own right. Pretty
soon she has become only an accomplice in Dulcie's doings,
and the relation she is made to enter into with a mid-European
Jewish knitwear salesman is treated with a condescension that
is discomforting. Indeed Viola is in the end dismissed from the
narrative: 'Viola had turned out to be a disappointment. . . . So
perhaps it was not surprising after all. Viola was just a rather
dull woman, wanting only to be loved' (ch. 17). Laurel is not
treated with the same contempt, but neither is there a great
interest in her, and her relationship with the young florist Paul

is merely a token presence. Most disturbing is the handling of Aylwin's wife, Marjorie (who, interestingly, does not appear in the early notes for the novel). The type is new in the novels: 'the fair-haired young woman wearing a mauve twin-set . . . fluffy shoulder-length hair . . . nearer thirty-five than twenty-five':

> As Marjorie handed over the partially wrapped donkey Dulcie noticed that she wore a gold wedding ring engraved with a design of little flowers. Her fingers were rather stubby, with childish-looking short – perhaps bitten? – nails. It suddenly occurred to Dulcie that Aylwin Forbes had married beneath him. (ch. 9)

Something might be made of Marjorie and her plight but the potential is not developed. Her reactions to what is, after all, the breakdown of her marriage are subordinated in the narrative to those of her comic mother, Aylwin's mother-in-law, Mrs Williton. Her capacity for feeling is denied:

> Marjorie opened her favourite women's magazine and turned to the serial, hoping to lose herself in it. . . . She had reached a state of apathy about her marriage, and her feelings towards Aylwin were a mixture of fear, dislike, and boredom. (ch. 20)

(Though this is perhaps the only sensible reaction to Aylwin in the novel.) Recalling that her former boyfriend had described her as good 'like bread', Dulcie reflects that perhaps Marjorie is the 'fancy cake' (ibid.) and nothing in the narrative allows her to be more. When, in a contrived scene, Dulcie overhears the terminating discussion between Aylwin, Marjorie and Mrs Williton (ch. 22), she is surprised at Marjorie's tears at the end of her marriage. It is difficult to know whether the surprise reflects on Marjorie or Aylwin, but it certainly reflects on Dulcie, in a way that the narrative seems not to intend. After that, Marjorie is easily dispensed with: she is said to have run off with a man she met on the train.

Dulcie's relation to the narrative voice is very close. Of course this close relation between a favoured female character and the narrative exists in other of the novels, but here, with conscious artifice, Dulcie becomes not a character who is a novelist, like Catherine Oliphant in *Less than Angels*, but a figure of the novelist herself. She is in *The Driver's Seat*, to use the title of Muriel Spark's self-conscious novel of 1970. Dulcie shares with her creator a taste for detecting: she likes 'finding out about people' (ch. 1). She is compared to a novelist (ch. 7) and is almost able to produce the appearance of characters: 'The concentration of one's thoughts on a particular person can sometimes have the effect of making him appear, and so it was on this occasion' (ibid.).

Self-conscious elements multiply as the narrative proceeds. Pym refers to her own works (among the novels in Dulcie's house is *Some Tame Gazelle*). Life is compared to a novel: 'Perhaps there was some kind of pattern in life after all. It might be like a well-thought-out novel, where every incident had its own particular significance and was essential to the plot' (ch. 10). For Dulcie the story is 'like a kind of game', an opportunity 'to observe their joys and sorrows with detachment as if one were watching a film or a play' (ch. 12). As the narrative takes us to the West Country hotel of Aylwin's mother this kind of element begins to predominate over all others. There is no action in much of this part other than Dulcie's researches into the Forbes family, in which the reader does not have the same interest, and which have no issue. Here Barbara Pym 'herself' enters the novel:

> It was at this point that somebody came to the unoccupied table, but as she was a woman of about forty, ordinary-looking and unaccompanied, nobody took much notice of her. As it happened, she was a novelist; indeed, some of the occupants of the tables had read and enjoyed her books, but it would never have occurred to them to connect her name, even had they ascertained it from the hotel register, with that of the author they admired.   (ch. 18)

Wilmet, Rodney, Piers and Keith from *A Glass of Blessings* are brought on for a turn: again there seems little point, other than to draw our attention to fictiveness, and one rather resents the manipulation to this end of the characters from the earlier novel. Finally, the ending of the novel, when Aylwin comes to Dulcie, is compared to the notoriously unsatisfactory ending to *Mansfield Park*, where Austen tells rather than shows us that

Edmund's affections have transferred themselves from Mary Crawford to Fanny Price.

One of the consequences of this investment in self-conscious fantasy is that the novel lacks poetic texture. *No Fond Return of Love* is weak in description, and there is a strikingly small number of literary allusions. Aylwin is named 'after the title of the famous novel by Theodore Watts-Dunton', the man who 'incarcerated' the poet Swinburne (ch. 9), but it is difficult to see why and the allusion has no reverberation. The nearest thing to a focusing image the work provides is the stone squirrel in the front garden next to where Marjorie used to live with her mother when Aylwin was courting her. The squirrel is mentioned repeatedly, and then it is gone: 'the squirrel had disappeared. He felt a moment almost of panic and began looking in other parts of the little front garden to see if it had been moved elsewhere' (ch. 21). But the image declares itself inadequate as a focus of feeling. As the action is switched, in a rather broken-backed way, from London to the seaside in the West Country, Aylwin makes an effort to generate a poetic expression of feeling, remembering the lines of Matthew Arnold, 'so appropriate to human relationships in general and to his own in particular',

> Yes! in the sea of life enisled,
> With echoing straits between us thrown,
> Dotting the shoreless watery wild,
> We mortals live *alone*.

But he cannot rise to the sentiment: 'it was less noble than that – his relationship with Marjorie and their drifting apart. Nothing in common but a stone squirrel, he thought derisively' (ibid.). Later he feels that 'even the stone squirrel seemed ridiculous and embarrassing when associated with Marjorie' (ch. 22). As an image the stone squirrel signals the failure of, and even resistance to, emotion. These feelings extend beyond the relation of Aylwin and Marjorie to the novel as a whole.

No Fond Return of Love thus represents a crisis and turning-point in Barbara Pym's art. What it particularly draws attention to is Pym's narrative method. Pym usually adopts a narrative position very close to the central emotions and even fantasies of her central characters. In keeping, her narrative style is not marked off from the pleasant, deceptively simple style of the conversation of her central characters.

The continuity of these elements from novel to novel is a factor in how we read them. It is a false purity to pretend that readers do not have favourite authors – especially if the author is like Barbara Pym – and that the perception or construction of an author is not part of the reader's pleasure. Hence the consciously self-alluding elements in *No Fond Return of Love* only draw attention to an effect that is already felt, for with Pym's fiction the reader necessarily interprets a particular kind of authorial involvement. One does not need to know *A Very Private Eye* to imagine that Barbara Pym was like her narrative voice and central characters, and there is nothing in her fiction to suggest that one should or would be likely to develop some concept of an authorial persona, behind which there is an unknown author painting her fingernails.

Pym is closer to Trollope in her narrative methods than to many modernist authors – the Trollope who was concerned in his narrations that the reader should be treated courteously and not be subject to hidden attitudes or tricks of withholding information. Trollope, however, based his fiction on self-overcoming and kept himself further out of his fiction than Pym does. The sense of the continuity between romantic-novel writing and the maintenance of romance in life is part of the appeal of novels such as Barbara Pym's, especially the sense that this attitude is something shared among women. The publication of *A Very Private Eye* is therefore, despite its title, continuous with the kind of interest Pym's fiction generates. The editors, Hazel Holt and Hilary Pym, clearly recognised this fact.

The reader, therefore, does not need the conscious artifice of references to novel-writing, the novelist and the earlier novels to feel a particularly pleasing and intimate relation with the author. It is one in which privacy is still maintained as it is between people who share an unspoken preference for expressing themselves by referring outwards with wit and sympathy to the life around, rather than directly inwards to the hungry heart. *No Fond Return of Love* violates this contract, because it is not in this sense social enough, and therefore the usual pleasure of relation with its author is less present. The author does not bear herself as well in this text, and, though we are in a sense closer to her, we feel at a greater distance because what is revealed – a demand on life, and the relative subordinating of life to that demand – is something from which we are bound to feel somewhat apart.

Barbara Pym's are novels of manners in a different sense from, say, Jane Austen's, for in Pym the question of manners enters into the very relation between reader, narrator and characters. Austen presents manners, and stands back in so doing. George Eliot, for her part, conducts a prolonged three-person relation between reader, narrator and characters, but the sense of the narrator's wisdom and authority is great, and the relation is hardly one between equals, or, at the least, it has not the ordinary acceptance of our little desires, feelings and needs. Pym is a romantic novelist, she writes about our romantic feelings, and she brings characters, reader and author close together in this shared recognition of what romance means to our lives, with all its potential for confusion, disappointment, humiliation, and comedy. But this recognition needs to be sustained by a certain manner, akin to the manners that her characters demonstrate, a maintenance of tone and style which is not just style but the expression of self-forgetfulness and thoughtfulness about others.

We do not follow the Pym narrator or her characters into the bathroom or the bedroom, but, because we know such places exist (unlike in certain Victorian novels, where there is a real doubt as to whether they exist at all), there is the potential for comic or embarrassed awarenesses. Pym's novels take place in public spaces – streets, restaurants, churches, libraries, offices – but a few pages of any of them will convince us that the most private rooms, and their equivalent places in our imaginations, are much closer than in Austen or Eliot. There is just that hint of a recognition of bodily function; the chance that someone may appear in a corset or in tears; the necessity of seeing food prepared and not just consumed; the bathroom under the stair with the toy soap in it; the contents of other peoples' bedroom cupboards and drawers; the whiff of sexual desire. In so far as her novels take place largely in the public rooms of a house, they do so in smaller and less formal houses, or in flats, where the more private areas are always quite close: as in a bed-sitting room where the couch folds down as a bed, or a kitchen where the washing can be seen drying. Pym delights in this order of forced and unmentionable intimacy.

It is questionable whether we can be much more intimate with a novelist and her characters: such things are, after all, more intimate in the day-to-day sense than ecstasy or agony. If the reader is offered in a narrative the contemplation of the most lurid sexual intimacies, he or she is addressed only to the end of excitation, intimacy of a limited kind. D. H. Lawrence was once seen to offer a deeply vital and shared relation between author, characters and reader, but really most of us do not live like that, and, anyway, what is shared in a Lawrence novel, other than a certain excitement, often seems to be a rather external stridency. We may conceivably come out of a Lawrence novel feeling invigorated (or spent?) but we are unlikely to feel very close to each other: we have only marched to the sound of the same trumpets. With Pym, the music is more like chamber music, to which we can all contribute our parts in a shared expression and form: a quartet, perhaps, or a common hymn-singing, like that at the end of *Some Tame Gazelle*, when we are all singing together our hopefulness, well-meaning and desire for happiness.

The narrative mode of *No Fond Return of Love* is therefore a sign not of intimacy, but of distance. The novel is the sign that Pym's fiction was moving into a new and less certain phase in which there is an increasing sense of strain, demand, and unbridgeable gulf in adult love relations. This is what *No Fond Return of Love* has in common with its successors, *An Unsuitable Attachment* and *The Sweet Dove Died*. It is clear that even before the rejection of *An Unsuitable Attachment* Pym found this new way of writing more difficult and demanding, and she was far less certain of her intentions and effects than she had been in the earlier comedies.

An Unsuitable Attachment

This is the problem with the rejected novel, *An Unsuitable Attachment*, the first version of which was written between 1960 and 1963, but which was rejected by Cape in 1963, revised between 1963 and 1965, and not finally published until 1982. The work is undoubtedly very uneven, but it contains more interesting characters and is richer in texture than *No Fond Return of Love*. Its most obvious faults are those Larkin recognises, the undecided and unconvincing account of the relationship between Ianthe and John, and the unnecessary indulgence of the introduction into the novel of characters from the early novels. In addition, like *No Fond Return of Love*, the novel is divided between a home and holiday setting, a North London suburb and Italy, and, though there is a far-reaching thematic effect in the juxtaposition, it is somewhat obscured by scenes of sub-Forsterian comedy of the genteel English abroad, in which the novel barely seems to tick over.

The little notebook for *An Unsuitable Attachment* (MS Pym 20) is of great interest. On the first page, after recording the birth and death of her cat Tatiana, the model for Faustina, Pym listed some possible titles:

A Heart Inside
Under the Lemon Trees
Books at the Heart
A Marbled Page
A Box of Sweets
A
The Marbled Lemon
Wrapped in Lemon Leaves

Whether this list was made before the notes that follow or not, it is interesting that a number of these titles refer to the scene between Sophia and Ianthe on the balcony of Sophia's aunt's home. There follow a number of neat character sketches of principal characters: Sophia, Mark –

> Mark, Sophia's husband is rather remote, the kind of man who cannot be helped (rather like Walter)

and this note about Ianthe:

> Just to glimpse her big toe protruding (like some exquisite tortoise head?) from a sandal seemed almost too great an intrusion of her privacy

Of John she asked, 'How can I bring such a person within my range?' The ideas for him are a little wild:

does he work for the vet?
has he been in prison for embezzling or passing dud cheques
no – have him work at the library
does he have a hairstylist brother with a contempt for
    women?

Other notes begin to establish the post-imperial elements in the
novel: of Agnes, Pym observed, 'Espousing good causes, rather
out of date. Release Dr Banda!', and she made the note 'the
Union Jack on the vicarage line?'

Pym then drafted an opening to the novel, set at the country
home of Sophia's mother, where the theme is the 'falling off' of
modern life, which the domineering old woman knows nothing
about. There follow a number of pages about the North London
setting, in which the focus on this area is established. Among
these pages there is the note

> In Sophia's corner of London – perhaps – it is just off the
> Harrow Road – a little group of sympathetic people are
> collected. Into this group comes John, the alien, pretending
> to be one of them.

Two things are interesting about the notes thus far: one is the
continued radical uncertainty about John; the other that the
novel is still told from Sophia's angle rather than Ianthe's. In
the final version much more is given to Ianthe's point of view,
and that, in turn, leads to the acceptance of John and some re-
evaluation of Sophia.

Notes for the Italian scenes of the novel occur about the
middle of the notebook. There is a sketch of the scene at the
villa where Ianthe talks about her love, in which Sophia's
remoteness is indicated (she is thinking about her cat), but the
image of the lemons and the details of her aunt's circumstances
are not included. Other ideas for the Italian scenes then follow,
including the fine comic one that Rupert will call Penny a 'jolly
little thing'. Pym was still unsure about John, sketching an
uneasy last chapter and toying with the idea of his having an
embarrassing uncle and aunt. The last notes in the book,
however, are again possible titles:

> The Arch of Leaves (Swinburne)
> Laurel is *green for a season* and love is sweet for a day

Among the lemon leaves
The Sycamore leaves –
A Friend for Sophia

Again the list of titles suggests that the scene at the villa is somewhere at the heart of the novel's feeling.

The characters of *An Unsuitable Attachment* are, and largely remain, unattached. Ianthe Broome is a genteel, prim but handsome librarian. She conceives a feeling for her socially-lower fellow librarian, John, or, rather, responds to his show of attention to her. In the event they are rather unconvincingly married. Meanwhile Mervyn, the head of the library, entertains a very limited feeling for Ianthe which leads to an unromantic proposal, and a neighbour, the anthropologist Rupert Stonebird, also proposes to her. In turn, Penelope Grandison, sister of the local rector's wife, is in pursuit of Rupert, who may by the novel's end intend to pay attention to her. Along with these very limited developments there is the marriage of the rector, Mark Ainger, and his wife Sophia, which is curiously defeated. Thus, as the relation between Ianthe and John is 'not done', as Larkin says, and that between Rupert and Penny is at the very best half-hearted on his side, the sense of unrelatedness and the failure of relationship prevails. It seems as though Pym was reluctant to go along with this, however, since she sacrifices probability to romance in relation to Ianthe and John.

Larkin remarks that the novel is the most churchy of Pym's works, but this is misleading in two respects. First, there is not the sense of the community of the church that there is in some of the earlier novels. There is a church outing – the trip to Italy – but that does not create the effect of community, rather the reverse. Second, unlike *Some Tame Gazelle* or *Jane and Prudence*, the parish is not a pleasant country parish, but an urban parish in North London, and the evocation of the urban scene and the changes it portends is much stronger than the limited recognition of changing lifestyles in *A Glass of Blessings*. This is one of the novel's strengths:

This was the very fringe of his parish, that part that would never become residentially 'desirable' because it was too near the railway, and many of the big gaunt houses had been taken over by families of West Indians. Mark had been visiting, trying to establish some kind of contact with his exotic parishioners and hoping to discover likely boys and men to sing in the choir and serve at the altar. He had received several enthusiastic offers, though he wondered how many of them would really turn up in church. As he walked away from the house, Mark remembered that it was along this street with its brightly – almost garishly – painted houses that Sophia had once seen a cluster of what she took to be exotic tropical fruits in one of the windows, only to realise that they were tomatoes put there to ripen. 'Love apples,' she had said to Mark, and the words 'love apples' had somehow given a name to the district, strange and different as it was from the rest of the parish which lay on the other side of the main road, far from the railway line. (ch. 1)

The parishioners who go to Italy are not drawn from the parish as a whole, just from the immediate clerical circle. Their relation to the remainder of the parish is suggested by the manner of Sophia when confronted with a caller: 'Sophia rubbed her skirt and hands with a towel and composed her face into the patient sympathetic mask she wore when confronted with one of her husband's black parishioners' (ch. 20). The novel presents not churchiness but the borders of genteel life and other realms.

The suggestion of strain in Sophia's response to an unfamiliar world is explored more fully in relation to Ianthe. At Christmas, Ianthe visits a retired employee of the library, one Mrs Grimes, in another district of London. Mrs Grimes mistakes the violets given to Ianthe by John as a gift for herself, and the whole experience of the woman's worldliness is disturbing to Ianthe's Christian motives. Later she makes another descent into this alien world, this time to John's lodgings when he is ill:

They were standing in a narrow hall, with a bicycle propped against one wall and stairs leading down to a basement. The floor was littered with papers – coupons offering '3d off' soap powder and frozen peas, and literature about television insurance and reconditioned sewing machines – which had evidently been thrust through the letter box. There was no sound in the house, apart from what might have been the twittering of a caged bird coming from one of the closed doors on the ground floor. Then a kind of muffled shouting could be heard somewhere underneath them, as if somebody was having a fight or an argument. Ianthe felt tired and rather hopeless. (ch. 10)

The person she is with is an irritated and unhelpful clergyman making his visits:

> She had not liked him very much but she judged him to be one of those unfortunate men who dislikes their neighbours even more than they dislike themselves and as such he was to be pitied, plodding on from day to day among his bingo-playing telly-watching parishioners. (Ibid.)

Upstairs there is the blare of television advertisements; an Asian family; John's cheerless room, 'a sink and a gas ring, partly hidden by a screen, a pile of unwashed crockery on a small table and a red plastic bucket filled with empty tins, tea leaves, and broken egg shells' (ibid.).

Ianthe's personal primness is thus placed in disturbing contexts. Larkin is surely mistaken to place the novel among the earlier comedies, for the sombreness he attributes to the later novels is very present here. Ianthe's house has a wintery effect about it, 'the garden now piled with drifts of sycamore leaves' (ch. 2). The violets she is given at Christmas also have a cold chill about them: 'Their cold fresh scent and passionate yet mourning purple roused in her a feeling she could not explain' (ch. 6). Pym suggests elements in her past which are chilling and inhibitory, notably a disapproving mother. When she is kissed at the station prior to her departure for Italy, an experience which she is not used to, Pym employs a suggestive device to dramatise the shock:

> Ianthe hurried on to the escalator and began walking down. At the bottom the warm air blowing about her seemed to increase her agitation. A piece of newspaper was swirled about her legs and she collided surprisingly, almost nightmarishly, with a nun. (ch. 12)

This develops to suggest her mother to her memory:

One did not behave like that in a public place with a young
man, suitable or otherwise, and John was so very much
otherwise. It was not surprising that at this moment the
image of her mother – the canon's widow in the dark flat
near Westminster Cathedral – should rise up before
her. (Ibid.)

It is understandable why Pym's basically optimistic art could
not countenance the failure of the relationship with John, for in
Ianthe she created a character who was capable of real and
even tragic pain at such an outcome. Ianthe has a grace of
manner and bearing to which a number of characters attest:
'Ianthe's absolute rightness here – the Englishwoman in Rome –
in her cool green linen suit and straw hat' (ch. 16). But there is
something naked and vulnerable about her perfection:

There was a delicious smell wafting from a pink hyacinth
which was growing in a glass on the table at his side. It
seemed typical of Ianthe, the slightly schoolmistressy touch
of growing the bulb in water so that its white Medusa-like
roots were visible. (ch. 16)

An imagery gathers about Ianthe: she is the vulnerable princess
of a fading way of life. Her qualities make her, unlike Sophia,
open to the larger world that the novel introduces; her central
fear makes her singularly ill-equipped to cope with that world.
    Therefore it is equally clear why Pym could not successfully
imagine any relationship with John. She wished to use him to
give her heroine a possibility in which she could not herself
believe. Even his name, Challow, suggests qualities such as
'callowness' and 'shallowness'. Some of the problem is the
consequence of Pym's own naïveté: wearing pointed shoes and
reading Tennyson are hardly as incompatible as she seems to
think (the author of this study has done both), and it is her own
ignorance to assume that a man who has been an actor, and is
now a librarian, would not know the name of the Trevi fountain.
John borrows money from Ianthe when he is ill, and Pym is
uncertain whether to have him pay it back, or show himself up
by not doing so: it is uncertainty, rather than the desire to keep
the reader in suspense. At the final wedding-scene John and
Ianthe are both shadows (earlier we have seen John putting up

shelves in Ianthe's house, as though he were incapable of conversation), and Pym still toys with the suggestion that he might be revealed as an imposter, even be denounced at the wedding as Jane Eyre's Rochester is. This is narrative sophistication masking real emotional confusion.

One way of describing the new urban evocations in the novel would be to say that the sense of the world beyond Britain, the 'anthropological' imagery as it were, is present in a new way. It is not simply a matter of comic play, as in *Some Tame Gazelle*, nor is it organised into a strict ironic system of oppositions and correspondences as in *Less than Angels*. Rather it is diffused and dispersed into the scene: in other words, it escapes the term 'anthropological' and becomes part of the post-imperial return of the Commonwealth on the British centre. In the earlier novels, as well, there is a clear opposition between anthropological and novelist's visions, respectfully distanced and sympathetic imaginings of society, though the two are brought together in the *tour de force* of *Less than Angels*. However, in *An Unsuitable Attachment* they are not only brought together but collapsed into each other: ' "Haven't the novelist and the anthropologist more in common than some people think?" said Everard' (ch. 11). The anthropologist Rupert Stonebird (the surname an allusion to the phallic stonebirds of Zimbabwe) has recently regained his faith; some of the 'churchy' characters, if they have not lost theirs, have lost something like faith. Oppositions of distance and togetherness are not so easily made: distance is within, and the novelist's position is less assured in its feelings.

Early on in the novel there is a fine image of its emotional and historical nexus, one of those interesting scenes in Pym in which a woman observes something from a window. The density of the evocation here is typical of the best writing of this novel:

As she watched, Daisy saw Sophia come out into the garden with Faustina in her arms. The cat looked like some great noble bird, a hawk or even an eagle, the golden streak down her nose giving the effect of a beak. She struggled from Sophia's embrace and jumped down among the windfall apples, rolled one over with her paw, then turned and stalked indifferently away among the Michaelmas daisies. Sophia went back into the house and came out again with a bowl of washing, from which she shook out a large Union Jack. This she draped over the line, pinning it with a row of clothes pegs.

Wherever did she find that, Daisy wondered, that symbol of Empire. What rare objects, what richness, the attic of a vicarage must hold! Probably not many in this neighbourhood or, for that matter, in any other would have a Union Jack on their clothes line. Of course one didn't say Empire now, but Commonwealth – common weal, weal and woe . . . Daisy's thoughts wandered inconsequentially. Then she saw Sophia go over to the statue of the Virgin Mary. Was she about to make some obeisance to it? Daisy leaned forward, at once horrified and fascinated. But no, she was removing the blue drapery, and now, with that gone, what had seemed to be a popish image turned out to be merely a tree stump with a blue cloth spread over it to dry. The shape and fold of the cloth had suggested a draped figure.

Sophia now picked up Faustina again and went back into the house with her. She makes too much of that cat, Daisy thought, for a young woman that is. It was a pity she had no children . . . .   (ch. 2)

The cat, Faustina, brings together much of the novel's sense of things. Cats suggest a certain ruthless amorality:

As she passed the vicarage she was startled to see Faustina picking her way along the front wall with a palm cross in her mouth. How unsuitable, she thought censoriously, though of course the crosses had not yet been blessed.   (ch. 10)

Faustina is the point of contention between Mark Aigner and Sophia, the sign of the absences and distances in their relationship. She is, as well, with her imperial name, a subtle link between the English scenes and those in Rome.

However, as has already been suggested, much of the potential of the Roman scenes is dissipated, though some of the comedy of unattachment is attractive. But the counterpointing of reactions is not successful and the introduction of characters from the earlier novels is simply distracting. Ianthe, too, is here reduced by the requirement that she should begin to fall in love with John: she is made to think, 'Now there is a whole ocean between John and me' (ch. 13), which is bad geography, and even wishes that she may return to Rome with her love when she throws her coin in the Trevi fountain (ch. 15).

The most interesting scene in Rome, where the potential of the scene for slightly unreal holiday romance is explored, is between Mark and Sophia. There is something missing in their relationship. Mark, we are told, has 'never seemed quite real' to his sister-in-law, Penelope. He has 'that remote expression sometimes found in the eyes of sailors or explorers', and a hankering after celibacy (ch. 1). On one occasion, Sophia has vaguely expressed her sense of dissatisfaction to Ianthe: ' "I'm the sort of person who wants to do everything for the people I love and he is the sort of person who's self-sufficient, or seems to be . . .". "Then there's Faustina." ' Ianthe is comically shocked by this comparison between cat and husband, but she is not wrong to sense that something is really wrong, for the chapter ends with Sophia alone in 'the cold church, making some effort to get into the right mood for the service. God is content with little, she told herself, but sometimes we have so little that it is hardly worth the offering' (ch. 8).

In Rome, Mark and Sophia almost have a moment of connection:

'I was thinking that an obviously romantic setting has something to be said for it. I suppose I don't love you any more here than when we're walking in Ladbroke Grove – how romantic *that* might sound to a foreigner, by the way – and yet it seems as if I do.'

'But *do* we walk in Ladbroke Grove?' Sophia murmured (ch. 14)

The moment passes, and the narrative follows the vaguely dissatisfied Sophia on her journey down to Naples with Ianthe to visit her Italianised aunt, who replaces the very British mother of the early notes. This aunt lives at the Villa Faustina: here the enigma of the Faustina factor will be explained.

The scenes at the Villa Faustina are among the most effective in the novel. Seen largely from Ianthe's point of view, they restore her to a role in which complex feelings are possible, and they display the other really interesting and complex character

in the novel, Sophia. The lemon groves, alluded to in many of
the titles Pym considered, are sensuously beautiful but carry as
well a suggestion of something concealed and unpleasant:

> The trees were covered with matting so that the fruit was
> almost hidden, but Ianthe could feel that there were hundreds,
> perhaps thousands, of lemons hanging there among the
> leaves. All those lemons, she thought, Sister Drew would say
> that they almost gave one the creeps.   (ch. 17)

A 'strangeness and homesickness' begin to invade Ianthe:

> even Sophia seemed different – not the vicar's wife but a
> stranger who appeared to be quite at home, and could speak
> and understand the harsh unmusical Italian of the south.
> 'You *must* see the lemon groves,' she had said.   (ch. 17)

Ianthe begins to discover in Sophia an alienation from English
values of domesticity, church and care, a taste for the life of the
senses, and a cynicism witnessed by her tolerant attitude to her
aunt's affair with an Italian doctor. Ianthe finds a tawdriness,
unpleasantness and a lack of love in such a vision of life. The
details that suggest this are nicely handled and the balance
between the moods and attitudes of the two women is well
maintained. The scene is all the more effective for the fact that
it reveals a growing distance between them: Sophia has seen
Ianthe as a rival to her sister, and has her own private and
elusive sense of things; Ianthe is trying to cling on to old values
whilst considering risking them to maintain them. It ends with
a faint feeling of dislike between these two excellent women.

There is also a blankness in the prospect. When Ianthe
decides to mention her affair with John, Pym writes, 'They
were leaning on a stone balustrade, looking out towards the
sea. Why shouldn't she tell Sophia, Ianthe thought, the beauty
of the view and its unreality overwhelming her' (ch. 17).
Unreality of one kind or another seems to overwhelm both
characters and even the novel itself, as though values and
possibilities were fading. In the conjunction of this unreality
with the blue distant beauties of the scene, Pym achieves an
effect something like that at the end of Philip Larkin's great
poem of the disillusionment of, and perhaps release from, desire:

And immediately
Rather than words comes the thought of high windows:
The sun-comprehending glass,
And beyond it, the deep blue air, that shows
Nothing, and is nowhere, and is endless.

('High Windows')

The chapter ends with Sophia:

And now here she was alone, unwrapping another little
bundle of lemon leaves to reach the deliciously flavoured
raisins at the heart, and feeling that this trivial delight was
almost enough to have brought away from a visit to Italy.

This is the latest version of the contrast in Pym between women
who achieve a relation of love, or at least a cherishing of lost
love, and those who form a relation with food: here the novel's
pattern of imagery and description gives a far greater reach and
suggestiveness to the detail. It is curious and unsatisfactory,
though revealing, to see Sophia try to apply the image to the
supposedly achieved relationship of John and Ianthe: 'The
lemon leaves had been unwrapped and there were the fragrant
raisins at the heart. She imagined John and Ianthe talking
happily together and tried to feel glad for them' (ch. 22). The
application entirely lacks inevitability: there is no way in which
the order of sensuality suggested by the raisins could address or
release the essential fears and needs we have seen in Ianthe. *An
Unfortunate Attachment* leaves us with a disturbed feeling. Its
comic and romantic drift of events seems, like the view at
Naples, to leave something out. And it is in this hardly placeable
sense of emptiness and pointlessness, its evocation of detachment,
that *An Unsuitable Attachment* is, for all its faults, a most
interesting novel about a phase of English life.

The Sweet Dove Died

The Sweet Dove Died was written between 1963 and 1969, but
was not published until 1978, after it had been revised for

publication in 1977. It had been previously rejected by a number of publishers, one of whom remarked that it was not the kind of novel in demand at that time; this was despite what Hazel Holt and Hilary Pym call its 'consciously stronger theme'. *The Sweet Dove Died* is, indeed, one of the harshest and least comic of Pym's novels, and its achieved artistry may be taken as the culmination of this period of Pym's work.

The achievement was not easily arrived at. Pym wrote two versions of *The Sweet Dove Died*. The first (in two drafts, MSS Pym 27 and 28) is set mainly in a country village, with a rich cast of eccentric characters, including a retired sociology professor who lives in a hut at the bottom of his former wife's garden; a failed and pathetic actor; a clergyman with a dominating mother; and a Pym heroine, Rose. Phoebe is a more dignified character; Leonora plays a smaller part and succeeds in fending off the threat to her world represented by Ned. The second version (which also exists in two drafts, MSS Pym 29 and 25) is the novel as we have it now. The change was brought about by Philip Larkin. Pym sent Larkin the typescript of the first version. Larkin felt that the story of Leonora was at the imaginative centre and that much of the rest of the material was redundant. He wrote, 'I think all the characters but Leonora, James, Humphrey, Ned and Miss X are irrelevant and should be dropped except for "comedy & pathos" ', and added, 'I think it would be a strong, sad book, with fewer characters & slower movement. Leonora is the chief character – I wonder did you feel sympathetic towards her?' Unsurprisingly then, *The Sweet Dove Died* has some of the coldly formal qualities of Larkin's two novels *Jill* and *A Girl in Winter* (which Pym had read).

One consequence of Larkin's intervention was that Pym decided that Leonora would not triumph. The notebook for the novel (MS Pym 26) divides into two parts. The first thirty pages are notes towards the first version of the novel. Then Pym made the title 'Notes for New Version' (fo. 31v) and followed it with the entry 'Leonora must have a woman friend/plain looking/(not Liz) who has a young man, more blatantly homosexual than James so that L feels superior but is ditched in the end just the same'.

The processes of Leonora's humiliation now begin to suggest themselves:

the afternoon at Keats's house
A showdown between James and Leonora
It isn't that I don't love you
the word 'love' had not been mentioned ^{between them} before

And, 'It would be artistically more satisfying if Leonora were to break down in front of Meg, whom she has always despised. So that Meg can be quietly triumphant' (fo. 39r).

Pym considered a number of titles: 'A Younger ^{twelfth} Man'; 'Not Subject to Return'; 'Prisoners and Captives'; 'Grapes in the House'; 'Object of Virtue'; 'Coveted Objects'; 'Objects of Desire'; 'The Triumph of Leonora'; 'The Growing Boy' (with the note, 'Shades of the Prison House begin to close / Upon the Growing Boy. Wordsworth'); 'Marble Men'; 'The Pyrrhic Victory'; 'The Red Turn Gray'. The title *The Sweet Dove Died* is from Keats, but the novel is largely unallusive and unpoetic in its texture. The heroine, Leonora Eyre, certainly has romantic names, but they are too insistent:

> 'I think Miss Eyre took it, Miss,' said the man stolidly.
> '*Jane* Eyre?' asked Jennifer. 'I don't like the sound of *that*.'
> 'Miss Leonora Eyre,' said the man. 'Unusual isn't it, that name, Leah-Norah.'
> 'Those Leonora overtures,' went on Jennifer gaily. 'I never did like Beethoven. The mixture of that and Jane Eyre is rather *disquieting*, don't you think?'   (ch. 10)

Like some of Pym's sympathetic heroines, Leonora has a taste for Victorian poetry, but with her the Victorian expresses not so much a sensitive personal life as the cultivation of appearance:

> The wide bed with its neo-Victorian brass headboard was conducive to pleasant thoughts and Leonora arranged herself for sleep. No Bible, no book of devotion, no alarm clock marred the worldly charm of her bedside table. Browning and Matthew Arnold – her favourite poets – took their place with her Guerlain cologne, a bottle of smelling salts, soft aquamarine paper tissues, a phial of brightly coloured pills to relieve stress and strain, and presiding over all of these faded photographs of a handsome man and a sweet-faced woman in late Victorian dress. Leonora had long ago decided that

her grand-parents were much more distinguished-looking than her father and mother whose photographs had been hidden away in a drawer.   (ch. 2)

Since Leonora's bedroom is not shared, for she has some of the fear of sexual intimacy of Barbara Bird in *Crampton Hodnet* and Ianthe in *An Unsuitable Attachment*, the image of herself that the objects create is for no other; it is a mirror. In the earlier novels the Victorian poets had connected with an interior life: here they are brought towards a world of objects; and objects, not books, provide the basic imagery of the novel, which is much concerned with antiques. Leonora, for instance, meets the other two main characters, Humphrey and James, at an auction; Humphrey runs an antique shop where James works; and the exchange of antiques marks all the stages in the relationships. It is in keeping that, when Leonora is deprived of the desired companionship of James, she prefers looking after objects to people or pets. The detail of the replacement of her parents' photograph by that of the grandparents is also telling, for, as we saw in Chapter 2, Pym normally associates the Victorians with a continuity of sentiment and responsibility. Leonora, who can evict an unwanted old lady from her flat, has nothing to do with what is, in Pym's view, essentially Victorian.

The one poetic text that runs through the novel, the lines from Keats that provide the title, is first quoted to Leonora by Ned, the unpleasant and egotistic young American academic who is depriving her of the attentions of James:

'The dove, of course.' But again the poem eluded her. Ned began to quote,
'I had a dove and the sweet dove died;
And I have thought it died of grieving . . .'
'Ah, yes, of course, that sad little poem.' Leonora was relieved that it was something so simple and harmless. Whatever had she expected? 'It died,' she said rather foolishly. 'Would you like some more tea?'
Ned passed his cup and went on with the verse, his voice lingering over the words and giving them a curious emphasis.
'O, what could it *grieve* for? Its feet were *tied*
With a single thread of my *own hand's* weaving.'

(ch. 18)

The poem comes to her as a cruel taunt and serves only to disturb her feelings, for she is unable to cope with the truer relation to the affective self that poetry implies. The visit to Keats's house in Hampstead is equally disturbing, for it is on this occasion that Ned forces a situation that demonstrates that James has chosen him rather than Leonora. Ned is cruelly manipulative, first intimating to Leonora that he and James are lovers, then taking possession of James as they walk round the house, then implying Leonora's age by insisting that she must be tired. Following this, he invites James and Leonora back to his rooms in Kensington (near the Brompton Oratory). Leonora is finally sent home in a taxi while the two lovers remain and her humiliation is complete.

The use of homosexuality is harsher and more explicitly sexual than in *A Glass of Blessings*, but this is only one aspect of the novel's hardness and distance from warm feelings. There is, for instance, no connection with the church in any of the characters' lives. It is a novel that is largely loveless and lonely. Feelings are selfish. The character who connects the others in the novel is James, who is Humphrey's nephew, the object of Leonora's attentions, then of those of a younger woman, Phoebe, and finally of Ned's. Ned in turn drops James and returns to America. On his very calculating advice, James attempts to make things up with Leonora, but she rejects his approaches. Her achievement is to break with him, and not allow herself to be used, but it is a rather mean and self-defeating victory:

> She and James had both been hurt, but it hardly seemed to make a bond between them – it was more like a barrier or a wedge driving them apart . . . the sherry they were drinking now seemed actively hostile in its dryness, inhibiting speech and even feeling. (ch. 25)

This is not the first time that Leonora has rejected emotion. On the occasion of James's first departure (ch. 21), when he moved out of the basement flat she had provided for him, he attempted a clumsy expression of feeling. It is understandable that it would be difficult for Leonora to cope with, but her attitude is, typically, to cut off emotion; the scene contrasts well with the scene in *Less than Angels* when Tom expresses his feelings for Catherine as he is leaving her.

Leonora has the same difficulty with the expression of sexual

desire. Her parents were consular officials and she has travelled:
as Pym remarks, with nice irony, she has had romantic
experiences in most of the famous gardens of Europe, and is
capable of being a little tedious on such subjects as Lisbon.
Here in England she is taken to the suitably named Virginia
Water, the scenery of which pleases her until she is disturbed
by 'a huge totem pole, shattering the peaceful beauty of the
landscape' (ch. 5). The introduction of this detail is not subtle,
but the idea is clear. Thus when Humphrey makes an advance
she reacts with fear and horror: 'He is going to kiss me, Leonora
thought in sudden panic, pray heaven no more than that. She
tried to protest, even to scream, but no sound came' (ch. 11).

Leonora is in the line of Pym female characters who carefully
preserve themselves from intimacy whilst cultivating romantic
relationships, a line which includes Wilmet in *A Glass of
Blessings* and is best represented by Prudence in *Jane and
Prudence*. What is interesting is that this novel (in its second
version) is given over so completely to that type: Leonora has
none of Wilmet's ingenuous capacity for real feeling, and there
is no character who is developed as an attractive alternative in
the way that Jane is in *Jane and Prudence*. The kind of woman
that Leonora is has difficulty forming friendships with other
women because she has difficulty in accepting her own feelings.
During her desolate days while James is pursuing his affair
with Ned, she takes a weekend visit to the home of an old
woman friend to attend a party. The occasion is reminiscent of
Wilmet's weekend visit to Rowena's in *A Glass of Blessings*, with
the differences that Leonora cannot help showing that she feels
left out; cannot form a relation with her supposed friend; and,
having retired to bed, is the subject of a disparaging conversation
between friend and husband. It is clear to her that she will not
return. During the same period she meets and can make
nothing of a female cousin.

Her reaction to her rival, Phoebe, is equally telling. Phoebe is
painfully willing, gauche, and open about her feelings. In a
novel where a high premium is placed on elegance and manner,
she is an inevitable victim. Her uncouth vulnerability and
directness give Phoebe such attraction as she has: it lies in the
pathos of her availability. It is also what makes her failure
predictable: she has no allure, or self-possession, that could be
the basis of a continuing interest. As such she makes a nice foil

to Leonora, though the gap between them is so complete that there is no point of contact except when Leonora repossesses James's furniture from her. The transaction is conducted through the willing Humphrey, and the only sight Phoebe has of Leonora is of the elegant woman in sunglasses in the back of the car. This is the greatest distance between women, even women who are rivals for the same man, we have yet seen in Pym's novels, for the scene lacks even the comically direct hostility of Jessie Morrow to Prudence in *Jane and Prudence*.

Leonora does have women friends of a sort, but they are women who have recognised that they must love, whereas Leonora does not mean to love without control. One is Liz, another of Leonora's lodgers, who was unhappily married to a man who was, in an unspecified way, 'appalling', who now devotes herself to a flat full of cats, and who likes to disect her marriage and remark on 'All that love, *wasted*' (ch. 7). The sense of defeat, hurt and bitterness under the show of independence is apparent, and Leonora can only relate to Liz by way of contrast.

Meg is the 'woman friend' introduced in the notes for the second version. She is in her fifties, and 'devoted' to Colin, a homosexual man in his twenties: ' "Most of Colin's lovers" – she brought out the word courageously – "have been rather different. He's had *such* unhappiness . . ." ' (ch. 2). Dependence becomes all too clear at Christmas – always a difficult time for Pym's world of aging singles – when a distraught Meg calls on Leonora in tears, looking such a sight that Leonora 'averts her face' at the prospect of an unattractive and needing woman. Colin has not been to collect his present; he is cold and evasive; he is not answering letters. Leonora is brisk:

'I shouldn't worry,' said Leonora. 'You make far too much fuss of Colin, you know.'
'But he's all I've got,' Meg cried, her voice breaking.
Leonora turned away in distaste.   (ch. 4)

When Meg next appears she has learnt the lesson of the episode: ' "You have to let people be free," said Meg, in the brave manner in which she had spoken of Colin's "lovers". "In that way they come close to you" ' (ch. 7). Leonora is still confident she can keep her bird caged, but it is, anyway, a lesson she will be unwilling to learn in the way Meg has learnt it, for that is to be broken and humbled by need. Meg even finds medical justification:

> 'Apparently it's really good to interest yourself in a younger person, a sort of child substitute,' Meg went on, 'everyone *needs* to love. One should just let one's love come flowing out, Dr Hirschler said' – here Meg gesticulated with her arms – 'not bottle it up or be ashamed of it.' (ch. 20)

It is, as Pym realised, appropriate that Leonora should in the end give way to her feelings in front of Meg. But the gap between the two women remains. Leonora's sense of irony and distaste for Meg's sentiments remain. She cannot accept Meg's code of acceptance and 'noble and unselfish sentiments'. Her refuge is self-possession.

The novel is thus one of Pym's bleakest explorations of certain kinds of women's love. We have seen that Pym frequently employs a pair of women: Jane and Prudence are the obvious examples. One adopts a relation to men of distance which perhaps has fear at its centre; the other accepts need, but experiences some diminishment in doing so. In the earlier novels Pym was able to imagine romantic possibilities for both these responses. In *The Sweet Dove Died* they are equally failures. This seems to be more than the recognition that a single woman at fifty is vulnerable and may become lonely: it is the exploration of the inevitable defeat of certain kinds of structures of female affectivity – indeed, more or less the available range as Pym presents it. The novel provides an analysis of the limitations of certain roles and identities for women, for what these women, Leonora and Meg, have in common is the inability to be themselves and be in a romantic relationship.

The Sweet Dove Died is also a novel of the growing loneliness of age. At Meg's dinner party early in the novel, Leonora meets the uninspiring Harold, Colin's latest lover, who is a vet's assistant, and who has, Meg enthuses, lovely strong hands. When Leonora later thinks of death, Harold comes into her mind:

> For a moment Leonora dwelt on the idea of Colin's friend Harold, imagining those strong kind hands putting animals to sleep. Certainly one didn't want to think about *that*. Yet

there was no reason why one's death should not, in its own way, be as elegant as one's life, and one would do everything possible to make it so.   (ch. 2)

The investment in objects and appearances in the novel may thus be seen as a form of preparation for death. Leonora's vision of Harold here carries through the two possible female responses to a male world (for here the male looms as large as the veterinarian to the pet): go to sleep in the firm hands, as Marcia does in *Quartet in Autumn,* or arrange one's own elegant death. It is also one sign of the imminence of time. One of the most well-calculated scenes in the novel is when Leonora must go to the dentist (ch. 11), to have two fillings: even the exquisite teeth are going. The dentist is, of course, an admirer; he also collects antiques. The experience leaves Leonora feeling sick and faint. To recover, she promises herself tea in Wigmore Street, and 'one of her favourite cakes . . . lightest foundations'. The subtle suggestions of time, death and deep-seated panic in this passage are fine: even the cake Leonora wants has been taken when she arrives. *The Sweet Dove Died* thus points to the world of the aged in *Quartet in Autumn.*

For all this the novel has its limitations. The withdrawal of a warm centre of feeling and search for values is a loss. In its detachment, the novel suspends or omits certain kinds of interest and involvement with the characters. They are thus, in a measure, uninteresting. It is not always easy to care about Leonora, who, for much of the novel, seems simply elegant and selfish. As has been said, we do not see a lot of the other female characters. Humphrey is very much the foil. James, the object of attention, is insignificant other than as a good-looking young man: this is an intentional irony, but it prevents us from interesting ourselves in him or his relations. Phoebe is painful, Ned well observed but unpleasant. It is not just that we are detached, or that Pym is: the consequence is that none of the characters has quite the vivid reality and individuality of characters in the earlier novels. Pym has denied them too much. To withdraw comedy is to withdraw seriousness in Pym: the seriousness of involvement. The novel is much better constructed than either of the two earlier attempts at more distanced fiction discussed in this chapter; whether it is as rich and interesting as *An Unsuitable Attachment* is another question. It partakes of the world it evokes: it has the air of the well-

designed room that nicely exhibits its contents, not the feeling
of a place lived in.

An Academic Question

Something must be said here about the academic novel, of
which Pym wrote two drafts in 1970 and 1971 before abandoning
it to begin work on *Quartet in Autumn*, and which was
subsequently edited by Hazel Holt and published as *An Academic
Question* (1986). The book was a conscious attempt to write a
kind of novel that Pym perceived to be in vogue ('a sort of
Margaret Drabble effort' she called it in a letter to Larkin), but
Pym had no experience of provincial universities and her
handling of academic rivalries and meannesses has none of the
intimate comedy of David Lodge or the controlled unpleasantness
of Malcolm Bradbury, the two most successful writers in this
vein. Her heroine, Caroline, is married to an ambitious middle-
ranking academic. She steals some papers from the chest of a
dying man at a nursing home so that her husband can advance
his research at the expense of his elderly professor and then
must find a way of ensuring that the act is not discovered.
During this episode she discovers that her husband has had a
brief sexual liaison with a woman who works for his publishers
in London. There are no grand consequences, only an ironic
diminishment of everyone's aspirations, but Pym is clearly
unhappy with the attitude she attempts to adopt and the
required suspension of feelings and values. She created an
unpleasant university world somewhat in the vein of some of
her lesser contemporaries and then found she could not come to
terms with it. None of the characters is drawn with great
conviction, though the racily named Iris Horniblow, an
ambitious, sexually insecure woman academic, is nicely
observed. More interesting is the introduction of an elderly
woman character who has begun to remove herself from
connection with life, concerning herself instead with feeding
hedgehogs: such an 'eccentricity' is developed in the Miss
Liveridge of *A Few Green Leaves* and far more dramatically in
Marcia in *Quartet in Autumn*: Pym had begun to imagine total
withdrawal. Hazel Holt has done a great service in providing
Pym's readers with *An Academic Question*, but it is unlikely that
the book will ever be a favourite.

5

Language and Loneliness: The Late Novels

Alongside the novel 'after Joyce', as represented by the novels of Beckett, Robbe-Grillet, Handke and others, there flourishes a novel that seems to possess continuity with what is loosely called nineteenth-century realism, which continues to employ recognisable and ordinary scenes and characters, and which is apparently indifferent to the searching questions about language that preoccupy the 'post-Joyceans'. This continuity is particularly evidenced in England, where flirtations with literary modernisms in the 1960s and 1970s were both short-lived and relatively superficial. There *is* a parochialism about contemporary English culture, but acknowledging it does not explain the survival of the traditional form, or something like it, not only in England but in most cultures where the novel has flourished. It might simply be argued that what characterises the post-modern is diversity (and that there is correspondingly much greater diversity within the tradition than the use of 'traditional' here suggests). So much may be admitted, but it leaves the problem of the applicability of contemporary literary theory, which has developed in close alliance with modernist forms, to the normative tradition. If that understanding is not applicable, or finds little of interest to say when presented with texts of this order, are we to conclude that such texts embody a general lack of sophistication and, in particular, a limited, even naïve, unawareness of the problematics of language itself?

The novels of Barbara Pym are fine recent representatives of the traditional novel form, presenting a recognisable novel world in which her readers clearly delight. What can contemporary criticism say about such a novelist as Pym? Is she simply employing a 'realism' which, from the heights of critical theory, can be seen to be epistemologically naïve, just as her 'world' is quaintly 'irrelevant' to the world that normally offers itself as relevant? Obviously one response to this kind of view is to reject in turn, as Philip Larkin rejected modernism and all its doings. But it is worth trying to answer the questions posed by modernism and critical theory, for we can better appreciate the fiction of Barbara Pym – just as we can that of Robbe-Grillet – if we can perceive something of its implicit epistemology, or, to put it another way, its argument about language and world.

Language is posed as a problem in the modernist text: in the work of Beckett or Robbe-Grillet or Handke. The declaration made by the forms of the works of such writers might be briefly and inadequately summarised as follows. Language is a system that has no intrinsic relation to reality, but which is determined by certain structures: texts emphasise this view by their dislocations of normative time–space relations and perspectives. The possessor of this language is alienated from 'nature' or any order of things, including the nature of others and his or her own nature. The individual is, in fact, more possessed by than in possession of language: the individual is only the locus of these structures and an attendant desire or *Angst* to transcend them. His or her isolation from other language-bearers is an inevitable consequence of unfulfilment in language, though it may be added that what is often represented as particularly galling to the bearers of such experience is the individual naïve enough to believe in the communication value of language: this is a recurrent frustration and joke in Beckett, for instance.

Evidently none of this applies to Pym's world, which seems to exist within 'ordinary' language usage far from these isolations. One way to begin to establish her 'poetics' would be to begin with the 'friendly' and 'conversational' quality of her works, what A. N. Wilson (1982) has called their 'gossipy' quality. This conversational manner certainly establishes a normative narrative world, but its very intimacy and chattiness does not create the sense of a narrative separate from and aligned to a supposed reality in a mirror fashion. The modernist or post-modernist text gives us more of the impression of being an object set over and against the reader, and, while not mirroring the world, it retains, even as it denies, the mirror relation to it: it is, it might be said, an opaque mirror, or text-object in the place where the presumed mirror of the so-called realist text was. As such, it is fixed at the point of the assumed epistemological problem: of the non-relation of language to world, sign to signified. This accounts for the circling quality of Beckett's work and the obsessive gaze of Robbe-Grillet's, for instance. By contrast, a novel by Barbara Pym does not fix us at this point: in its conversational mode – the product of a certain style and attendance on the experience of a central character – it does not in any strict sense 'represent' a world. Rather it introduces aspects of the world within the context of particular human needs and activities as such elements are introduced in conversation.

To employ the characterisation 'conversational', however, is to run the risk of opposing voice to writing, an opposition of which Derrida has made us very wary. It may be argued, though, both that the opposition is rather one between a voice metaphor and a visual metaphor (the sign pictures/does not picture reality) and that the characterisation 'conversational' does not imply any of the metaphysics of 'presence' which Derrida attributes to the voice metaphor. 'Conversation' suggests the normal distances and limitations of language (Pym always makes us aware of what cannot be said in conversation), not metaphysical presence.

Barbara Pym's sense of language is better characterised by reference to Wittgenstein than by reference to Derrida. Wittgenstein was a philosopher much concerned with the limits of language. The movement of his philosophy was away from the picture view of language of the *Tractatus* (which argued a relation of logical to atomic simple) to an account, in his later works, of language in terms of language games derived from forms of life, in which ostensive definition is not typical of how language is acquired (see his criticism of language acquisition in Augustine) or anything but a rather peculiar and specialised language game. The development of Wittgenstein's philosophy from its early to its late phases also implied a changing attitude to the 'structure' of language, a change which is suggested by the shift from his favourite early metaphor for language, the game of chess, to an appreciation of the wide variety of language games we play, games which have no common essence or structure, but which can be linked by what Wittgenstein called 'family likeness'. 'Rules' now vary according to situations, and situations are manifold. For Wittgenstein, the sort of epistemological problems that preoccupy post-modernist fiction and post-structuralist criticism would be pseudo-problems, based on misconceptions of both philosophy and language, or, to borrow the view of the American pragmatist philosopher Richard Rorty, not solvable and hence not interesting.

Pym's fiction can clearly be related to the late Wittgensteinian account of language and language use. Such a riposte, however, does not imply for Pym an 'easy' or 'complacent' relation to language. Wittgenstein's own life and work, it has often been observed, suggest a pained awareness of the limits of language, and particularly of the absence of anything we can call an inner language, 'ourselves'. This awareness is akin to the sense of language we discern in Pym, whose narrative and characters are engaged in varieties of ordinary language games (one of which is telling stories, narrating) but which also make us aware of the extent to which language is unable to express what we feel, or might want to say, to overcome our loneliness. It might be said that in Pym language is felt as a limit, a not-ourself, rather more as manners are than as a philosophical problem, yet this statement would not suffice to catch the final sense of how her novels portray and are themselves representatives of creative fictional gestures that sustain hope and conversation in a world in which lives are increasingly adrift and in which hopelessness and silence always tug at the sleeve.

Once this is perceived it becomes clear that Barbara Pym's fiction is in a number of essentials different from its realist predecessors (reviewing *A Few Green Leaves* in 1980, Nicholas Shrimpton wrote, 'Where Austen was a Romantic miniaturist, Pym is a 20th-century minimalist'). First, it is noticeable that she employs many literary allusions in her works, or her characters do. These allusions function to suggest an intertextuality, repetition and hence textuality such as realism eschews. But it is also striking, as was observed in the discussion of *Some Tame Gazelle*, that the effect is very unlike (say) the use of quotation or allusion in Eliot's *The Waste Land*, where every citation, while it renders the surface life unreal, reinforces or echoes a structuring text. Instead, quotation and allusion in Pym have a wry function: author and characters are aware that quotations from literature epitomise but also glamorise life, which cannot attain to the same degree of concentration, expression or even presence – hence the taste for minor authors and passages, which are 'more like us' as it were (the pursuit of minor authors is finally paradoxical, since what one seeks is the literary non-literary, and what one arrives at is a deliquescence into ordinariness).

Secondly, as we have seen, Pym introduces characters from one work into another, but the effect is rather different from that in the novels of a 'chronicler' such as Trollope, for in Pym their presence is a sign of fictiveness. We have also seen that in the novels of her transition period Pym, perhaps influenced by her English contemporaries, experimented uncomfortably with self-referring fiction (Chapter 4). This was an error, but its existence and its lack of necessity in her work both point to the manner in which she always reminds us of the gesture of language. Like the reintroduction of characters, the phase of self-referring fiction is only an explicit sign of the feeling her novels give us of the author or characters *creating* interest in life and appealing to the same tendency in the reader.

It has also been suggested that, despite her similarities to her nineteenth-century predecessors such as Austen and Trollope, Pym does not have the same relation to social authority (Chapter 2). Along with the loss of social authority went a loss of the shared-world confidence that provided the literary authority that underlies nineteenth-century realism. Rather than presuming a shared world, Pym's fiction enacts the seeking of some part of it. It was argued that the church, 'Victorian' and out of place in the modern world, replaces the image of the Victorian house in Pym's fiction. In addition, churchmen and churchwomen are repeatedly set against anthropologists in the novels. Though there is delightful comedy about both, Pym is clearly 'on the side of' the church, though her novels are far from being spiritually insistent. Indeed, it is the very banality and vague uselessness of Anglicanism that seem to attract her to it. The contrast with anthropology is more than a contrast between ambitious and selfish academics and nice unworldly types, though it includes that: it is the contrast between an ambition to a scientific or objective mode of observing mankind and a tentative, literary-related, sensitive, ethically based mode. Anthropology is arrogance to Pym, and a parallel can be made between anthropology in her work and the ambition of structuralism to see human productions such as language and literature objectively, as systems, from the outside (post-structuralism being only a complication). Wittgenstein rejected that kind of approach, seeking instead a more 'involved', attentive non-systematic kind of description, by which forms of life were validated. Pym's fiction is a parallel gesture, refusing to view literature as an objective mode of charting, carrying an implicit criticism of critical attempts to achieve that objectivity and, instead, emphasising the function of literature within forms of life. This involves the replacement of scientific pretensions by ethical concerns, the production in her characters and readers of the virtues of humour, courage, and the humility of the recognition of desire. The fond familiar old Church of England, a church which (in a widely held view) holds its beliefs and forms without dogmatic insistence or intellectual coherence, but which provides a proper realm for human niceness, hopefulness and folly, is an appropriate image of the house of language in Pym.

Finally, because Pym presents the problem of language within forms of life and not philosophically or absolutely, her works represent a testament to a particularly female experience of language. If modernism were to turn its eyes on this purveyor of hopeful commonplaces, then the image it might provide of her would be a little like the character Winnie in Beckett's *Happy Days*, whose banal, moralising, sentimental chatter, laced with a little asperity, attempts to fill the play's interminable stretches of time. But the play also provides, in the figure of the prostrate, seedy, and largely silent Willie, a telling representation of the male contribution. Like Beckett in *Happy Days*, Pym presents a world in which women do the thankless work, always experiencing the characterisation of their language as trivial, finally inadequate, offering only the banality of happy days. Pym all along associates anthropology and modernism with male arrogance; it might be argued that what is finally discerned in them is a refusal to feel in a world without ultimate meaning.

It is, however, primarily through her female characters that Pym explores the theme of language and loneliness. In *Quartet in Autumn*, the triumph of her last phase, she provides a memorable and profound exploration of a woman who withdraws from language and community, and in *A Few Green Leaves*, her last work, she presents a heroine equipped with an authoritative and distancing language, that of anthropology, who, in a sense, learns to become a novelist.

Quartet in Autumn: 'People Who Belonged Together in Some Way'

At the front of one of the notebooks for *Quartet in Autumn*, Barbara Pym placed a letter she had received from the DHSS (Department of Health and Social Security) indicating that, as she was still ill, she would continue to receive payments. The letter has a rubber-stamp signature. Pym had herself been in hospital, and another notebook contains a series of interesting jottings of her experience there, in the course of which she began to conceive the character of Marcia. And in the notes for the novel itself she wrote, 'Marcia can have been in hospital then I can use all my St Mary's bit.' The notes for the novel (MSS Pym 32 and 33, fos 79–91) are a deeply impressive testimony to Pym's acute awareness of her times, fixing the details of each of her characters' lives with wonderful perceptiveness. In many of them a fearful resistance to a changing world is registered: 'He didn't like the engine at the back of the car – it seemed unnatural like a square watch face.' Or: 'A woman slumped on a seat in the morning underground rush hour. Rather like somebody one had been to school with? But certainly it *is* her!' (fo. 86). This is improved in the final version: the woman, who has there collapsed in the underground station, looks like an old school acquaintance, but when she shouts out, 'Fuck off', Letty is sure she is not: only manner provides the certainty (ch. 2).

Pym then drafted about a third of the length of the novel as we have it, giving much more to Letty's past. She then broke this continuous narrative with a note that shows she had discovered the compositional principle of *Quartet in Autumn*: 'Episodic – short bits, but not jottings. They must be pruned from what is already there' (MS Pym 31). She next made a much-corrected draft typescript which concludes with the note '(This novel finished in its rough imperfect state, 1st September 1975)' (MS Pym 33–4). During the writing of this typescript she was experimenting with possible titles, and the list is interesting: 'Four wishes', 'Four lonely ones', 'A study in isolation', 'Alone, lonely, solitary', 'Solitude, thy lovely seals (?)'; 'The wingless ones (termites)'; 'Living alone'; 'Finishing alone'; 'Ideas for an Ending'; 'Four souls in solitude'; 'A Something else thereby'; 'A something of Four'; 'A Song of Four'; 'the Four in Solitude'; 'The Solitary Four'; 'Quartet in Finish'; 'A Short Time before the End'; 'Persons in Solitude'; 'Retiring Persons'; 'The Bubble of Solitude'; 'The Bliss of Solitude'; 'Keeping People Out'; 'States of Solitude'; 'The Fire was Sinking'; 'Sinking Fires'; 'A strange relationship'; 'Wandered'; 'No Social Contact'. When she sent the novel to Larkin he wrote, 'It's so strange to find the level good-humoured tender irony of your style unchanged but dealing with the awful end of life: I admire you enormously for tackling it, and for bringing it off so well' (MS Pym 152). But he understandably disliked the title, 'Four Point Turn', that she had settled on. Was Larkin responsible for the introduction of the word 'Autumn' into the title, with its suggestion of consoling and deepening natural processes? There is no hint of the sweet poetry of *Quartet in Autumn* in the titles Pym considered. If not, Larkin certainly contributed to the novel in another way. An aging bachelor, conducting a long-distance relationship with Pym; his published writings and letters much concerned with age and loneliness; addicted to denouncing the age and its works, as in the comment, only half-humorous, in a letter, 'I feel deeply humiliated at living in a country that spends more on education than defence' (18 March 1969) – Larkin is surely the source of some of the attitudes presented in the novel, perhaps especially those of Norman.

More memorably and completely than any previous works by Pym, *Quartet in Autumn* succeeds in creating a persuasive and penetrating imaginative account of contemporary England. Its achievement can be compared with the best of Larkin's poems, 'Ambulances' and others, and was surely in its tone and understanding influenced by them. With it, Pym completed the movement from her early comedies to a major statement about her civilisation, as E. M. Forster did in the movement from his comedies to *Howards End* and *A Passage to India*. It is a novel about age, but it is also a novel about the failure of a civilisation.

This failure is subtly and comprehensively registered, presenting itself more as a disturbance on the edge of reflection than as a direct thought. One register of this theme is the repeated references to Empire and post-colonialism in the work. 'How had it come about', Letty wonders, 'that she, an English woman born in Malvern in 1914 of middle-class English parents, should find herself in this room in London surrounded by enthusiastic shouting hymn-singing Nigerians?' (ch. 7). Empire itself has faded: 'Letty felt that the way things were going nothing was pink on the map anymore' (ch. 6); and the evidence of its return on the home nation is more comprehensive than in earlier works such as *Less than Angels* and *An Unsuitable Attachment*. Letty finds herself with a black landlord, Mr Olatunde, and the lively young black girl in the office is disturbing to the elderly quartet, but the novel is not a diatribe against such developments, for the inadequacy of the English reaction is too clearly presented: the sign 'KILL ASIAN SHIT' that appears on a wall is only an extreme manifestation of the bitterness that infects some of the central characters (ch. 2). Nor is it simply that the provisions of the welfare state are perceived as impersonal, well-meaning but wholly unable to address the central needs of the lonely, the aged and the alienated. The novel achieves its strength because the aged are seen not simply as victims of a state of affairs, but also as in some degree its purveyors and perpetrators.

After her retirement Letty passes the place where she had worked all her life:

> To reach the library she had to pass the office, and naturally she glanced up at the grey monolithic building and wondered what Edwin and Norman were doing up there on the third floor. It was not difficult to picture them at coffee time, and at least there would be nobody installed in her and Marcia's places, doing their work, since nobody was to replace them. It seemed to Letty that what cannot now be justified has perhaps never existed, and it gave her the feeling that she and Marcia had been swept away as if they had never been. With this sensation of nothingness she entered the library. (ch. 13)

The scene – the single figure in the street looking up at the large impersonal building – provides a familiar image of the indifference of the social order to the individual. But Pym's point is subtler: the sense of nothingness Letty experiences partly comes from within; it is something she and her aged friends have brought with them to the contemporary scene. Edwin, looking at a colourful range of 'girlie' magazines, again provides a juxtaposition that, while it makes the point about contemporary society, exceeds it: 'Edwin looked at them dispassionately. He supposed that his wife Phyllis had once had breasts but he could not remember that they had been at all like this, so very round and balloon-like' (ch. 5). This is a comment on Edwin and not just Edwin's age. When Letty dreams of a past lover, she is similarly disconnected from her experience: 'In Letty's dream she was lying in the long grass with Stephen, or somebody vaguely like him, in that hot summer of 1935. He was very near to her, but nothing happened' (ch. 2). On an earlier occasion, having failed to speak to a woman seated at her table in a restaurant, Letty accuses herself, 'It was too late for any kinds of gesture. Once again Letty had failed to make contact' (ch. 1). Ironically, the same phrase is later used by a social worker: 'A lot of them seem like that at first, but the contact has been made, that's the chief thing. And that's what we have to do – *make contact*, by force, if necessary. Believe me, it can be *most* rewarding' (ch. 3). Characters and institutions are linked in the same failure. The injunction '*make contact*' reminds one of Forster's nostrum for deep-seated contemporary ills: 'Only connect.' Contemporary England and the middle-class England of Malvern in 1914 are both judged. As the poet Tom Paulin remarked in 1978, 'Barbara Pym's work has now deepened into a formal protest against the conditions both of life itself and of certain sad civilities that no longer make even the limited sense they once acknowledged.'

It is the failure to connect that Pym presents between the central characters. There is a repeated motif of a gaze, which, rather than establishing contact, distances and reifies what is observed. Marcia had once felt 'a faint stirring of interest in Norman' and followed him at lunchtime:

> She found herself entering the British Museum, ascending wide stone steps and walking through echoing galleries filled with alarming images and objects in glass cases, until they came to rest in the Egyptian section by a display of mummified animals and small crocodiles. Here Norman had

mingled with a crowd of school children and Marcia had slipped away. (ch. 2)

The introduction of the children, and the choice of verb, 'mingled', are nice touches. The gaze is repeated when, after Marcia's retirement, Norman is led by feelings obscure to him to walk past her house:

He stood on the opposite side of the road and gazed in stunned fascination, very much as he had gazed at the mummified animals in the British Museum. . . . It was such a strange sight that he was as if rooted to the spot. He had a feeling that she had seen him and for an instant they seemed to stand staring at each other – again it was like the British Museum encounter with the mummified animals – giving no sign of mutual recognition. Then Marcia disappeared from view. (ch. 15)

What Pym shows in *Quartet in Autumn* is lives that have somehow not quite had the energy or emotion to bridge a gap, and which have, in numbers of small ways, become narrow, mean and self-defeating. The humour of the book is sad, derived from the littleness of what we can contrive to live by, and seem to prefer. Appropriately the texture of the novel is the least poetic in any of Pym's successful works. It does not offer a pattern of allusion and description that focuses in a deepening metaphor; rather it provides a metonymic texture of juxtaposed objects, like the string, bags, bottles and tinned goods that Marcia hoards. Similarly the movement between scenes suggests lives that are juxtaposed rather than connected.

Of the two central male characters, Edwin is the less interestingly developed. Churchy, stiff, prim, a house-owner, he is more or less contented with himself, and has sufficient idea of himself as a churchman (he dines with the priest) to make small interventions on behalf of his fellow workers, finding Letty, after her retirement, a room in the home of a wealthy single parishioners, Mrs Cook, and having a sense of owing something to Marcia, though its limits are nicely defined:

The parable of the Good Samaritan kept coming into his mind and making him feel uncomfortable, though it wasn't

in the least appropriate. There was no question of him
'passing by on the other side' when he didn't even go
anywhere near the house, and for all they knew, Marcia was
perfectly happy.   (ch. 15)

This is an amusing instance in the life of a character of the
substitution of the metonymic or contiguous mode of thought
for a metaphoric one.

The other central male character, Norman, is a considerable
achievement. He is repeatedly described as an 'angry little
man' and he has some of the bitterness about contemporary
English life that is discernible in the later work of the now
aging angry young men of British literature, such as Osborne
and Amis, and which is an explicit theme in the writings of
their greater contemporary, Larkin. This scene, for instance, is
reminiscent of Larkin's 'High Windows':

Norman gravitated towards the girls playing netball and sat
down uneasily. He could not analyse the impulse that had
brought him there, an angry little man whose teeth hurt –
angry at the older men who, like himself, formed the majority
of the spectators round the netball pitch, angry at the semi-
nudity of the long-haired boys and girls lying on the grass,
angry at the people sitting on seats eating sandwiches or
sucking ice lollies and cornets and throwing the remains on
the ground. As he watched the netball girls, leaping and
cavorting in their play, the word 'lechery' came into his head
and something about 'grinning like a dog', a phrase in the
psalms, was it; then he thought of the way some dogs did
appear to grin, their tongues lolling out. After a few minutes'
watching he got up and made his way back to the office,
dissatisfied with life.   (ch. 4)

Norman has struck a meanly triumphant little deal with life.
With the exception of moments such as this, it is a generally
effective deal in that it keeps him perky in a slightly jeering
way: Pym has perfectly defined a representative post-war type.
Food, as often in Pym, is a motif in this novel, and Norman's
satisfaction at his chosen diet of bacon and eggs, and his
favourite, butter beans, nicely expresses his style. His use of
language is a triumph of Pym's observation: ' "Up to you to

make a go of it," said Norman chirpily. That's the ticket." '
Such vulgar little phrases, stock in the language of his
generation, with their reduced sympathies, function for him as
little flags of self-approval. Visiting his brother-in-law, a driving-
instructor who dreams of establishing his own driving-school,
Norman overhears him laughing with his intended second wife
in the kitchen while they wash up:

> Larking about in the kitchen, Norman thought, hearing the
> sound of laughter, but he wasn't really envious, his attitude
> being 'sooner him than me'. When Ken had deposited him
> on his doorstep from his brand new buttercup-yellow motor
> car, Norman returned to his bed-sitting room – quite well-
> satisfied with his lot.   (ch. 10)

But, for all his jeering littleness, Norman has a kind of passion,
even if it takes the form merely of angry rejection: ' "The sexy
blonde and the bossy do-gooding bitch?" Irritation seemed to
add violent colour to Norman's way of expressing himself.
"Catch me asking *them*!" ' (ch. 24). Like Marcia, he is less
tiredly well-adjusted than either Letty or Edwin, and it is an
indirect relation between Norman and Marcia, product almost
of their extremity, that leads to such positive developments as
do occur in the novel.

Marcia Ivory is the other great triumph of the novel, a
penetrating study of semi-self-induced deprivation and isolation
that ends in death. Her decline (though it is not simply that)
into a suspicious and resentful privacy, neglectful of her
appearance, resistant to the well-meant if inadequate attempts
of voluntary social workers, hostile to her former colleagues,
and centred on the grave of her dead pet cat, and on the
hoarding of milk bottles, tinned foods, plastic bags and other
items, is evoked in compelling detail. She chooses the extreme
of minimal dealing with the world and her own life. Her self-
imposed starvation is compared at one point to the anorexia
nervosa which is often associated only with younger women
(ch. 15), but which can extend through whole lives, a social
illness that still goes largely unrecognised because its victims
withdraw from attention and are not the nuisance that those
suffering from, for instance, drug addiction and alcoholism are.
Pym's reading of Marcia is the only adequate literary study of

the anorexic other than Charlotte Brontë's self-exploration in the Lucy Snowe of *Villette*. Pym discerns at the deep hungry heart of Marcia's response an entirely private fantasy, which finds its occasion when Marcia undergoes a mastectomy performed by a surgeon named Mr Strong. This event becomes the centre of Marcia's life:

> she liked to talk about herself, to bring the conversation round to hospitals and surgeons, to pronounce in a lowered, reverent tone the name of Mr Strong. She should even, if it came to that, take some pleasure in saying 'My mastectomy' – it was the word 'breast' and the idea of it that upset her. None of these speeches and conversations dealing with her retirement had contained any references to breast (hope springs eternal in the human) or bosom (sentiments to which every b. returns an echo), as they might well have done had the deputy assistant director's speech been more literary.   (ch. 12)

The passage reminds of Edwin's failure of memory in respect of his wife, and of Letty's failure to love, and it is interesting that Pym here associates the excision of the breast with the absence of the banally cheering literary commonplaces that sustain so many of her earlier characters. Marcia's operation provides a disturbing image of what has been disconnected in the others' lives as well.

The background to a feeling about the self like Marcia's and the occasion for her compensating fantasy are brought together in one passage:

> Marcia had been one of those women, encouraged by her mother, who had sworn that she never would let the surgeon's knife touch her body, a woman's body being such a private thing. But of course when it came to the point there was no question of resistance. She smiled as she remembered Mr Strong, the consultant surgeon.   (ch. 2)

Marcia makes a kind of god, a solution to all, out of Mr Strong, and part of Pym's case is no doubt to suggest how the doctor has come to function in a secular society where once the priest functioned, a point she took up again in her final novel, *A Few*

Green Leaves, and which is found in the modern poets who seem increasingly to lie behind her work (for instance, the surgeon God in Eliot's *Four Quartets*, or, again, Larkin). More significantly, though, Marcia reveals a deeply impossible fantasy about abandoning herself to an ideal strong male figure (fantasy typically producing as its object only a banality). Before him, but only him, she is pleased, gracious, and grateful: only he may touch her breast, to remove it cleanly, a terrible metonomy for the satisfaction of desire. On one occasion, her most free and emotionally enriched, she boards a bus at night ('illuminated like some noble galleon waiting to take her on a voyage of discovery', an image that suggests yet another Larkin poem) and rides to Mr Strong's home:

> But it didn't matter, she thought, as she approached the house, for now she saw that it, like the bus, was brilliantly lit up – resembling a great liner in mid-ocean rather than a galleon, what she imagined the Queen Mary might have been – and that elegantly dressed people were alighting from cars and walking up the drive. The Strongs were obviously giving a party. (ch. 17)

Marcia's fantasy image of the ship is stolen from her, or, rather, she hands it over to privilege and wealth: the passage suggests how class and social inequities confirm her self-deprivation.

Marcia, old white-haired bag-woman that she becomes, all the same resembles, in her fear of contact and private fantasy, some of Pym's earlier female characters – Prudence of *Jane and Prudence*, Ianthe of *An Unsuitable Attachment*, Leonora of *The Sweet Dove Died*; as the woman who spies, a very private eye, she also resembles something in Pym herself. Not only is she partly drawn from Pym's hospital experience, but she is a deeply courageous reading of part of her creator. When her collapse takes her back to hospital, Marcia is disturbed that Mr Strong seems to be frowning at her (he is, of course, concerned at her condition):

> He always seemed to be frowning – had she done something wrong? Not eaten enough, perhaps? His eyes seemed to bore into her – the piercing eyes of the surgeon, did people say that? No, it was rather the surgeon's hands that people

noticed and commented on, like the hands of a pianist when, at a concert, people tried to sit where they could see the pianist's hands. But in a sense the surgeon was just as much of an artist, that beautiful neat scar. . . . Marcia remembered what her mother used to say, how she would never let the surgeon's knife touch her body. How ridiculous that seemed when one considered Mr Strong. . . . Marcia smiled and the frown left his face and he seemed to be smiling back at her. (ch. 19)

Only at this moment can Marcia abandon herself, because for her to do so is to die. And, of course, Pym herself can be discovered in the figure not only of Marcia but also of the surgeon–artist.

Marcia's death is the central focusing event of the novel, and it precipitates developments in the lives of the other characters which promise more for them than had previously been the case. 'Marcia's death had of course brought them closer together', Pym remarks, and with her cremation there is a release, in a constrained and ironic manner, of new orders of language, the imagery of flowers ('the eternal usefulness of flowers') and a passage of poetry of a kind:

> Dust to dust, ashes to ashes.
> Into the grave the great Queen dashes.
>   (ch. 20)

It is then revealed that Marcia has left her house to Norman, removing from him a cause of envy, and making him feel (the banality of the phrase is nice) 'like a dog with two tails' (ch. 22). Independently, events change in Letty's life, so that she and Norman can join Edwin in having 'a choice', 'almost a feeling of power' (ch. 24). In addition, Letty's friend who lives in the country suggests that she and Letty invite Norman and Edwin out, so that the novel offers some possibilities, even if its concluding sentence seems to make, as Larkin felt, too great a claim: 'life still held infinite possibilities for change' (ch. 24). These are external manifestations of the change that *is* brought about. As the surviving characters gather to divide Marcia's hoarded food, it is as though they have experienced a common release and declaration. Somehow – and it is difficult to define how – Marcia's death has freed them all from a tension, from an isolating, terrified and unspeakable demand. At the same time her death is a declaration that forces a kind of recognition of a commonness at the level of – however mean, frantic and grotesque – appetite and desire. No novel of Pym's, and only the rare exception among others, so deeply explores the strange ways in which 'people who belonged together in some way' do belong.

A Few Green Leaves

In the notebooks for *A Few Green Leaves* (MS Pym 35/2–3) Barbara Pym copied a quotation from G. K. Chesterton: 'We do not believe in nothing if we don't believe in God, we believe in anything and everything.' In the quick and confident jottings for character and scene, she soon discerned at the centre of this question of belief 'the rivalry between vicar and doctor' (fo. 11v), and introduced a parallel alternative in wondering whether to make her heroine an anthropologist or a novelist. These concerns are essential to *A Few Green Leaves*. The notebooks also show that Pym was conscious, as she was with *Quartet in Autumn*, of adopting a new non-linear narrative: 'You could have a series of sharp well written scenes rather than a long boring connected narrative?' In this the novel form comes closer to its original conception in the loosely connected jottings of the notebook.

Written during the years of her ill health, *A Few Green Leaves* was to be the last novel Barbara Pym wrote and was published posthumously. *Quartet in Autumn* is a London novel: the chapter in which Letty goes down to the country to visit her friend Marjorie begins with the sentence, 'A pheasant sat in the middle of the field, unconcerned as the train drew into the platform' (ch. 5) – a witty image of sleek complacency, or what Letty feels is somehow the cruelty of the comfortable English country world. All the same, it is with the promise of relations at least partly pursued in visits to the country that *Quartet in Autumn* ends. *A Few Green Leaves*, on the other hand, is a village-*cum*-country novel, and a subdued comedy rather than a tragedy, its main characters in early middle age rather than old age. It is in a sense, then, Pym's return to the territory of *Some Tame Gazelle, Jane and Prudence* and the excised portion of *The Sweet Dove Died*. But it is also, like *Quartet in Autumn*, a novel about contemporary England, intent on registering the quality of English life, and therefore something of what Letty obscurely felt about country life is felt in its world.

In its evocation of a contemporary texture, *A Few Green Leaves* is a success. Its weakness is that, unlike *Quartet in Autumn*, it does not succeed in greatly interesting us in the lives of its characters. This is partly because, instead of focusing, like the earlier novel, on a small group, it employs quite a large cast, some of whom seem merely sketched: the notes of Emma Howick, the half-hearted anthropologist who represents the principal point of view, sometimes serve as a substitute for a fuller presentation, as though they were Pym's own notes towards a novel, not the thing itself. But this points to the difficult ambition of the novel: Emma is not a novelist and she has not quite a sense of what there is to say about the life around her (or her own life). Pym's aim is to treat of an apparent nothingness, of lack of incident, of a pleasant blankness in which lives can be lived, and in which in an uneventful way events can take place. The risk she runs, to which the novel at times succumbs, is of allowing the narrative itself to drift into inconsequentiality. In turn, the novel reflects on this problem through its examination of Emma's attempts to seek something significant to write about.

Another point of connection with *Quartet in Autumn* is in the use of the figure of the doctor, who is here explicitly posed as a modern alternative to the clergyman. There are two doctors in *A Few Green Leaves*: the aging 'Dr G', Dr Gellibran, something of a 'character', a believer in life, babies and common sense; and young Martin Shrubsole (the name tells us a little), who is felt by some of the characters better to represent the new nostrum. Both the rector's sister, Daphne, and Emma go to a doctor for what can only be called problems of life, and for which there appears no other answer. Religion is certainly not the answer for Shrubsole, who regards his mother-in-law's periodic visits to the graveyard as unhealthy.

For the village, the doctor has an obvious function, which the rector, Tom, lacks. Tom is the pastor of a community that has defined him as largely an irrelevance. His parishioners fail to turn down the television when he ventures a visit, and effectively restrict him to the vague little circle of church-goers and middle-class characters in his part of the village: Emma; two young anthropologists, Tamsin and Robbie Barraclough; an ex-priest turned investigator for a good-food guide, the sleek and well-fed Adam Prince; a few of the aging village well-to-do. Nor do the denizens of the surrounding great houses, who open their gardens to church parties on certain days in the year, otherwise exist in relation to the church. There is thus a certain logic in the crude ambition of Martin Shrubsole's wife, Avis, to move the vicar into a small council house so that her family can move into the spacious and attractive vicarage.

As Emma discovers, the great bulk of the village community has little contact with the members of its clerisy (Coleridge's word): 'Most of the original inhabitants now lived in the council estate on the outskirts of the village and one didn't have much contact with them' (ch. 6). The traditional roles of her class are no longer relevant:

'No,' Daphne agreed. 'The village women have such marvellous things now. They wouldn't look at cast-offs – it's we who buy them. Of course it's all to the good,' she added, feeling that she ought to say something on these lines. 'There isn't the poverty there used to be.'   (ch. 7)

Tom, the rector, spends his spare time, and one guesses there is a good deal of it, looking for a rural past, and sometimes he questions local people about it. But the answers are unsatisfactory: the villagers have no 'past' before 1930 or thereabouts: 'Tom knew by "the past" she did not mean quite what he did' (ch. 8). And again:

Tom hadn't listened, turned the subject, asking her if she remembered some of the old songs they had sung when she was a girl. But all Mrs Dyer could contribute was 'Run, rabbit, run' and 'We're going to hang out the washing on the Seigfried Line' from the early days of the war, and that hadn't been quite what he meant.   (ch. 23)

A knowledge of the old ways is a pleasant pedantry:

'The villagers still have the right to collect firewood –
"faggots", as the ancient edict has it – but they're less
enthusiastic about that now,' he said.

'Most of them have central heating anyway or would
rather switch on an electric fire when they're cold,' said the
rector's sister Daphne.   (ch. 1)

Tom's particular interest is in deserted medieval villages, a
potentially poignant image of lost community and spiritual
centre (such as the Victorians made of the medieval world they
invented). But that past is too removed to operate as more than
a vague sense of loss, as the contraction of the term 'deserted
medieval village' to 'DMV' (as in 'Tom's DMVs') suggests.
The effect is akin to that in Larkin's 'High Windows', when he
writes of 'Bonds and gestures pushed to one side/Like an
outdated combine harvester', a double remove from the poignant
image of the reaper.

The pattern of events in the novel is largely confined to
Emma's class and has the quality of a daily pointless drift. This
is not to say that there are not events of a recognisable order,
only to say something about the nature of the eventfulness Pym
gives them. For instance, there is a Miss Vereker, who features
in the conversation of Tom and others, and whose name
becomes a kind of half-humorous refrain. As a former governess
in the local great house, Miss Vereker is a representative of the
past after which Tom hankers, and, as a governess, she is a
potential representative of the heroic neglected single woman of
the nineteenth-century novels to which Emma is connected by
name, if by nothing else. It therefore seems that Miss Vereker's
unannounced return to the village, and her still more dramatic
collapse during an overlong walk through the woods, where she
is discovered by Emma and Avice, will be an event of potential
significance. But nothing comes of it, or nothing can be made of
it: Miss Vereker recovers and simply goes home to the West
End; perhaps the largest consequence for the lives of the
characters is that she is found on what proves to be the site of a
DMV.

Nevertheless, this is an area of climax of its kind in the novel.
That night – and the disconnection of causes is telling – there is
a power-cut in the area, and another elderly lady, Miss
Lickerish, an eccentric adopter of animals, who resembles Dolly

Arborfield in *An Academic Question*, dies: 'some time during those dark hours the cat left her and sought the warmth of his basket, Miss Lickerish's lap having become strangely chilled' (ch. 28). Death points to a deeper strata of experience and need, and at this time Tom feels that he comes 'into his own' (ch. 29). But again no connection can be established, for the village, now felt as a village in some unreachable and perhaps distantly traditional way, takes over the event:

> When she got there she found that two smartly dressed young women, whom she took to be the nieces, were sitting in the front room, a rather formal type of parlour, barred to the cats and hedgehogs, preparing to receive the flowers. The nieces wore bright colours – nobody went in for mourning these days, Emma knew.   (ch. 29)

Tom's role is subordinate to a peculiar amalgam of superstition and secularism:

> Apparently, as Emma learned afterwards from Tom, it was customary for the mourners to be present in church on the Sunday after the funeral. These particular people would not be seen at a service again until the next funeral, marriage or christening.   (Ibid.)

The deeper events the novel offers are of a different order. On the walk with Emma, in the moments before they discover the collapsed Miss Vereker, there is one such for Avice, when she lets out her irritation at Tom's occupancy of the rectory: ' "There would be no need to leave here – not if we lived at the rectory." Avice's stick slashed so furiously at an overhanging branch that she might have been cutting down Tom himself' (ch. 27). Her husband, Martin, has experienced a similar urge to violence, dreaming of the death of his mother-in-law, who is one reason why there is the need for another house. These are 'nice' people's pent-up violences, and have no consequence. When Emma walks with Graham, a former 'lover', they pass an abandoned chicken house, a failed business, where there is a disturbing stench: 'It seemed curiously, even bitterly, appropriate to the walk she and Graham were now taking, to their whole relationship now fizzling out at the end of summer' (ch. 22).

Rather than providing focusing moments that explore the depths of the spirit, the novel offers these little disturbances to the surface, patches of unpleasantness.

The dreams of Martin and Avis, like those of Tamsin and Robbie, are otherwise wholly containable within acceptable modern aspirations. The novel provides three characters who seek something more. Daphne, Tom's sister, has an ache of desire: ' "One goes on living in the hope of seeing another spring," Daphne said with a rush of emotion' (ch. 1). Her comically incongruous dream, the product of holidaying, is of a more elemental life in Greece: 'She had just put a gooseberry tart into the oven and was wondering what to do with the bit of pastry left over, forming it into various shapes, flowers or animals' and then – significantly – 'miniature human figures that reminded her of the little Cycladic idols she had seen in the museum in Athens' (ch. 17). The irony of her restlessness with her position is that after Tom's wife died she had rushed to his side, an act which she regards as sacrifice of herself, but which is a subtle form of dependence on him, serving to prevent him from filling the place of his late wife with another love. The daily movement of Daphne's restless desire, which is experienced by Tom – such is the obliquity of her expression of it – only as an irrational moodiness and irritation, is finely followed in an excellent chapter. Rummaging in the attic – the lumber room – Daphne comes across a sentimental Victorian picture of a dog:

> When Tom's wife died, she had come running to his aid with no thought for herself. All these years without a dog! 'Thy Servant a Dog,' she murmured softly to herself, not like cats, with their cool, appraising, insolent stares. 'Passionately fond of animals,' was how Daphne might have described herself, if anyone had asked her, and how she now began to think of herself. Animals were better than people any day.   (ch. 7)

The idea of a hairy, brown-eyed loving companion cuts across Daphne's dream of the elemental Greek life. Tom is surprised when the conversation turns to dogs, and then by the turn it takes:

> 'I think I shall get a dog,' Daphne said, when Tom came back to lunch.

'A dog? Whatever for?'
'Oh, you know I've *always* wanted a dog,' she burst out.
'Have you? You've never said so.'
'Oh Tom, you know how passionately fond of animals I
am – always have been.'

Had he been selfish all along, he wonders? The incomprehension
between them, the inability to confess and connect feelings, is
nicely caught by the chapter's concluding detail:

> Delving in the jumble box, he took up 'Thy Servant a Dog'
> and contemplated it. Hadn't it been the title of a book by
> Kipling that had supplied that quotation? But Daphne
> wouldn't know, so all he said to her was, 'No reason why you
> shouldn't get a dog, is there? Why don't you do something
> about it?' (ch. 7)

What the dog is for is what Daphne can do nothing about,
though she does leave Tom to take a house with an old friend
in Birmingham where she can keep an animal. Birmingham,
the dreariest of English cities, is not Greece, and Daphne comes
to regret her decision, and to think of returning. In the novel's
last scenes we see this purpose being blocked by Emma's
mother and her friend, who have perceived in Daphne's absence
an opportunity for Emma with Tom. At the end, Daphne lives
nowhere.
  Tom's yearning is less demanding and gradually focuses on
Emma. The scene that most reveals his feelings is that where,
in a moment of inner revolt, he reflects that he does not want to
draw his ideas for sermons from the splendid old ladies of the
parish (ch. 25). He wants something else. Emma, the immediate
cause of his discontent with his lot, is only obscurely aware of
wants at all. It is interesting that Pym gives the work's central
point of view to a woman who has been indifferent to literature:
Emma has despised her mother's interest in the novel and has
no poetry (the juxtaposition of a country setting with an absence
of poetry can serve to characterise the novel's texture). In fact
Emma has been an anthropologist, and in her Pym collapses
together what have been in the earlier works the antithetical,
though overlapping, roles of novelist and anthropologist. As a
professional anthropologist, Emma has arrived at a point of

indifference, without ambition or sense of purpose, taking a desultory interest in the life of the village, which might be subject for a study, an interest which rapidly narrows to her own circle and then gradually drifts into the potential involvement with her own life:

> She remembered that her mother had said something about wanting to let the cottage to a former student, who was writing a novel and recovering from an unhappy love affair. But this was not going to happen, for Emma was going to stay in the village herself. *She* could write a novel and even, as she was beginning to realise, embark on a love affair which need not necessarily be an unhappy one.   (ch. 31)

For Pym, novel-writing always has a relation to the continuity of romance in life. In this, her last novel, she reaffirms this central tenet, and, by beginning with a heroine so ungiven to this view, she once again demonstrates the variety of approach she could bring within her art.

6

The Critical Reception

The critical reception of the work of Barbara Pym can be divided into two distinct phases: before 1977 and after 1977.

During the years that her novels were regularly published by Cape, Pym built up a loyal readership. Reviews of her work were generally appreciative, but usually brief, and her novels were often reviewed as one of a batch of works by a number of writers. There was, however, private encouragement. As early as 1953 Lord David Cecil, 'a total stranger', wrote to Pym, praising her characters as 'living and credible and likeable' (correspondence in MS Pym 148, fos. 1–27). In response to *Less than Angels*, which he later told Pym 'I like the best of all your books', he wrote that 'No other living novelist writes books that amuse me as yours do; they enlarge my imagination too, by introducing it to new worlds.' Cecil continued to see Pym as a representative of the true art of the novelist. After the publication of *Quartet in Autumn*, he was quick to point to the limitations of even appreciative reviews:

The few reviews I have seen were properly favourable: but not all that intelligent. Reviewers now seem to lack humour and also any knowledge or feeling for the *art* of writing, in which you are so eminent. Most of them seem to ramble on in a sort of solemn, lower middle-brow way about a book's social background and relevance – whatever that means. Most of the great novels of the past would have got short shrift from them.

Philip Larkin was another enthusiast. He first wrote to Pym in 1961, expressing his admiration for her work, and suggesting he write a review of her for the *Spectator*. The correspondence

(MS Pym 151–2) developed over the years into an amusing and affectionate exchange, which gave both writers the opportunity to play parts that they clearly appreciated: 'I really know little about provincial university life', Larkin wrote in 1971. 'As a librarian I'm remote from teaching, examining & research; as a bachelor I'm remote from the Wives' Club or the Ups & Downs of entertaining; as an introvert I hardly notice anything anyway.'

At the centre of the correspondence was Larkin's growing involvement with Pym's work. His initial appreciation had been for the early comedies, and very early in the correspondence he showed he had reservations about the turn her fiction was taking: he was doubtful, for instance, about reintroducing characters from earlier novels into *No Fond Return of Love*, though he saw it as an exercise of 'coincidence rather than Barchester', a nice distinction. When Cape rejected *An Unsuitable Attachment*, Larkin offered consolation, but, when sent the novel in typescript, he pointed out the weakness of the central relationship and remarked, 'I found myself not caring very greatly for Ianthe.' A year later, he wrote a long and encouraging letter which shows both his willingness to promote Pym's work and his deep personal appreciation of it:

> Once again I have marvelled at the richness of detail and variety of mood and setting. *EW* seemed better than I remembered it, full of a harsh kind of suffering very far from the others: it's a study of the pain of being single, the unconscious hurt the world regards as this state's natural clothing – oh dear, this sounds rather extravagant, but time and time again one senses not only that Mildred is suffering but that nobody can see why she shouldn't suffer, like a Victorian cabhorse. Don't think I've been concentrating on the dark side: *STG* is your *Pride and Prejudice*, rich and untroubled and confident, & very funny. John Betjeman was here a few weeks ago & we rejoiced over your work.

As we have seen, Larkin was responsible for radical changes in *The Sweet Dove Died*. Later he was greatly appreciative of *Quartet in Autumn*: 'It is so strange to find the level good-humoured tender irony of your style unchanged but dealing with the awful end of life: I admire you enormously for tackling it, and for bringing it off so well.'

During the years in which Pym failed to find a publisher for her works she dropped almost entirely out of the public eye (an exception to this neglect was Robert Smith's article 'How Pleasant to Know Miss Pym', published in *Ariel* in 1971). It was the publication in 1977 of a special number of *The Times Literary Supplement* that led to wider recognition. Lord David Cecil and Philip Larkin both named her the most underrated writer of the past seventy-five years, Cecil claiming that her works were 'the finest examples of high comedy to have appeared in England' during that period. Larkin wrote in the *Spectator* in 1977 that her novels gave 'an unrivalled picture of a small section of middle-class post-war England. She has a unique eye and ear for the small poignancies and comedies of everyday life.' The same year, Larkin also published an essay on Pym's work in *The Literary Supplement*. These pronouncements led to the publication of new Pym novels and the republication of the old. Pym's literary career and her works were widely discussed on both sides of the Atlantic. *Quartet in Autumn* was a finalist for the Booker Prize (Larkin was chairman of the selection panel).

After 1977, Pym's work was widely reviewed, though not always with great perspicacity. *Quartet in Autumn* was well received, and the reappearance of *Excellent Women* and *A Glass of Blessings* welcomed, but comment on *The Sweet Dove Died* was less friendly. A review in the *Spectator*, entitled 'Genteelism', opened with the sentence, 'It would have been kinder to have left Barbara Pym unrediscovered'; the narrative was 'deodorised', there was 'hardly enough substance . . . to fill a medium-length short story in a woman's magazine'. The reviewer, Paul Ableman, clearly wanted to say something about gentility and was unable to distinguish between Pym and Leonora. In *The Times*, Peter Ackroyd attributed the rediscovery of the novels to 'literary nostalgia': 'She is the archtypical lady novelist, whose work is just ironic enough to carry the burden of its tradition.'

The sense that it was the Pym revival rather than the novels that were being reviewed is inescapable in the reviews of the posthumously published *A Few Green Leaves*. In *The Sunday Times*, Bernard Levin, having summarised the 'Barbara Pym story', remarked,

It is the first of her novels I have read, and unless it is very untypical of her work, I cannot for the life of me understand what all the fuss is about; *A Few Green Leaves* seems to me thin, dull and very nearly pointless.

He concluded,

For some, it may well succeed in portraying the Heart of England; for me, I fear, it did little but reinforce my long-held belief that the best thing we could do with the countryside is to cover it with an even layer of asphalt.

The *Spectator* review, by Francis King, was much more about the revival than about the novel itself:

Those who effect this kind of rescue tend to describe the writer rescued with the same hyperbole that conservationists use of some building that they have saved from some bull-dozer. In the latter case, one reads such phrases as 'One of the finest examples of Victorian domestic architecture'. . . . In the case of Barbara Pym, one reads that she was 'an important novelist', that her two novels *A Glass of Blessings* and *Excellent Women* were 'the finest examples of high comedy to have appeared in England during the past 75 years', and that she had 'the wit and style of a 20th-century Jane Austen'.

The imagery of these reviews enables us to characterise them as representing a political position. They express the new conservatism of the era faced with a novelistic world in which they recognise the burdens of delicacy, care and gentility (the style of conservatism that in this period was branded 'wet'). Pym had run into the ideologues of the new right.

In particular, it seems in England to have become an offence to compare her to Jane Austen (as A. L. Rowse did in *Punch* in 1977). Even the author of her obituary in *The Times* pompously remarked that her qualities 'gained some reputation for her among the discerning. They also drew down on her the injudicious comparison with Jane Austen. Though this was nonsense, her exploration of her own fairly restricted milieu' – and so on. There are two reasons for comparing Pym to Austen:

one is that her novels of manners are in the Austen tradition, which they patently are. The other is to suggest that her achievement can be compared to Austen's, which it can, though Austen is the greater writer. Here is another critic, led to compare *Crampton Hodnet* to *Mansfield Park*, and then to repudiate the comparison:

> And since the current editions of her novels carry a comparison with Jane Austen, it might be worth pointing out some of the differences between the mirror and the major talent. However little you share them, Jane Austen does have values – and by values I mean something more than a sense of the status a particular income can support. With Pym there seem to be no values at all, only projected fears and eagerly awaited disappointments. She is obsessed with surfaces, with fabrics and foibles.
>
> (James Fenton, *The Times*, 1985)

One can see how these remarks might arise out of a reading of *Crampton Hodnet*, where, as has been said, Pym makes an uneasy and temporary alliance with the big house, but the generalisation is hardly justified: fidelity, humour, humility and courage are values. To pretend to be above one's age, and to share Austen's assurances and allegiances, is a position that the critic can assume more easily than the novelist. Marilyn Butler, in 'Keeping up with Jane Austen' *London Review of Books*, 1982), suggested that Pym's detachment, comparable to that of the functional anthropologists, is what separates her from Austen.

The criticism of *An Unsuitable Attachment*, published two years later, is notably freer of *parti pris*, despite the fact that Larkin's Preface recalled the whole question of the revival. In *The Times Literary Supplement* (1982), Anne Duchene, whilst observing that Larkin can be seen 'cheating a little', and noticing the weakness of the central relationship, finds an energy in the 'peripheral characters' and significance in the setting in 'a run-down part of London'. A. N. Wilson in the *Spectator* (1982) remarked sensitively on the sad themes of personal courage and humility, and the way in which 'food, often of a very ordinary kind, fills the consciousness of every character in the book'. Peter Ackroyd, in *The Sunday Times* (1983) now perceived the historical scope of Pym's work:

It is, I think, a vision of emptiness – of ways of life and belief coming to an end, of incipient decay, like the gaunt houses which hold new and alien tenants. At the close of his novel, Barbara Pym tells us that tears might seem 'quite fitting' in Rome – where faith survives – but 'would be quite otherwise in St Paul's churchyard at lunchtime.' Despite its sly humour and its carefully measured prose, this is a melancholy book.

The publication of *A Very Private Eye* in 1984 called forth numbers of appreciative reviews, delighted by the revelation of a vivacious and complex life: the picture of Pym as the snobby spinster, her own Leonora, could hardly survive. In *The Times Literary Supplement* (1984), Peter Ackroyd was led to make some perceptive generalisations about her work:

> More than forty years before, while she was an undergraduate at Oxford University, she had written in her diary, 'I had to decide between giving my face a steam beauty bath and doing *Beowulf.* I chose the former, and I think the result justified my choice.' It is the insouciance which is so comic here, since it is the insouciance which comes not from naivety but from a special kind of detachment. Pym's fiction manages a similar tone, when plangent lines from the more obscure seventeenth-century poets are introduced in the middle of inconsequential contemporary conversations: is the discrepancy comic, poignant or merely bathetic?

John Carey, in *The Sunday Times* (1984), was similarly acute:

> She is adept, in both novels and diaries, at identifying the separate levels upon which we strive to conduct life, and she enjoys pouncing on points where the levels get mixed up – the Shakespeare calendar hung in the lavatory; a nun in a telephone box; the pacemaker that has to be removed from the patient after death lest it should blow up the crematorium.

The 'Pym revival' in England led in 1978 to the publication in America by Dutton of *Excellent Women* and *Quartet in Autumn* and subsequently of the other novels. Pym's work and career were widely reviewed (including in *Time Magazine* and *Newsweek*). American reviewers were particularly appreciative of the presentation of Marcia in *Quartet in Autumn*, of her choice of a deadly privacy, and of the general sense in that work of an incipient nothingness. The order in which the novels were published in America assisted the recognition that Pym was a novelist capable of dealing with modern experience, even if the world of her novels was generally unfamiliar to the American reader.

Nor was the comparison with Austen as charged as it was in England. In the *New York Times Book Review* (1982), Mary Cantwell, discussing *An Unsuitable Attachment*, observed that

> One is most aware of Miss Pym's progenitor in her repeated use of the word 'party'. Jane Austen was forever describing a 'party', not a fête but a group of people embarked on an expedition or an evening's entertainment. Miss Pym's modest expeditionary group in Rome is a 'party', a handful of Church of England innocents abroad.

Cantwell went on:

> A British reader may look on them with shocks, and laughs of recognition; to an American, they are as remote in time and place as Margaret Mead's Samoans, and what is most pleasing about Miss Pym is that, like Dr Mead and Miss Austen, she regards the natives with a cool, dispassionate eye.

Pym's anthropological eye has been appreciated in a number of American reviews. Her ability to discern social patterns is admired by Edith Milton in the review of *An Unsuitable Attachment* in the *New York Review of Books* (1982):

> The novel's list of the unsuitable is splendid and endless. In their confusion about who they are and how they should behave, the characters eye each other, hoping to find out what someone else thinks about them so that they will know what to think about themselves. This does not help enormously, since what other people think is usually based much less on their insight than on their insecurities. Ianthe Broome, particularly, is perceived by the other characters in the way least useful to her: as the inheritor of all the graces of a time gone by, a creature who owes it to everyone's high opinion of her to keep herself as inviolate as a rare antique.

Her choice between her own instincts and everyone else's advice is the central tension of the novel, which begins 'They are all watching me, thought Rupert Stonebird', and which describes social intercourse as an interchange of constant, mutual misperception.

This American appreciation of Pym the anthropologist is also evident in Charles Burkhardt's academic article 'Barbara Pym and the Africans' (1983).

A survey in the *New York Times Book Review* at Christmas, 1982 indicated that three out of the eighteen prominent Americans interviewed were enjoying Pym's novels. The grace, charm and humour of her unfamiliar English world were undoubtedly part of the attraction for the American reader, but so were her insights into the way we constitute society. A *Barbara Pym Newsletter* is now published in America, and there have been book-length studies of her work: Jane Nardin's *Barbara Pym* (1985), Robbet Emmet Long's *Barbara Pym* (1986), Diane Benet's *Something to Love* (1986), and Janice Rossen's interesting *The Novels of Barbara Pym* (1987). Long's study provoked a hostile discussion of Pym's style of femininity from the Booker Prize-winning novelist Anita Brookner (whose own work has been compared to Pym's). It can safely be assumed that Pym will continue to be at the centre of much interesting critical discussion.

For this writer Pym's achievement places her alongside Philip Larkin as one of the undoubtedly important writers of the post-Second World War period in England. Both writers developed literary forms that effectively express the English experience of this period, including its limitations. Both experienced a sense of diminishment and loss in post-war society; neither was able to identify with the developments in English life that are usually associated with the 1960s: instead they made a sometimes pained comedy out of the recognition of their incongruity in the new circumstances. Unable to attach themselves to the continuities of marrying and 'having a family', both were finely sensitive to the difficulty of sustaining personal hope and value. Nevertheless, their witty and compassionate fidelity to ordinary English lives made them sensitive registers of a changing social texture. They represent what is best in a silver age of English literature.

Select Bibliography

WORKS BY BARBARA PYM

Some Tame Gazelle (London: Jonathan Cape, 1950; New York: E. P. Dutton, 1983).

Excellent Women (London: Jonathan Cape, 1952; New York: E. P. Dutton, 1978).

Jane and Prudence (London: Jonathan Cape, 1953; New York: E. P. Dutton, 1981).

Less than Angels (London: Jonathan Cape, 1955; New York: E. P. Dutton, 1980).

A Glass of Blessings (London: Jonathan Cape, 1958; New York: E. P. Dutton, 1980).

No Fond Return of Love (London: Jonathan Cape, 1961; New York: E. P. Dutton, 1982).

Quartet in Autumn (London: Macmillan, 1977; New York: E. P. Dutton, 1978).

The Sweet Dove Died (London: Macmillan, 1978; New York: E. P. Dutton, 1979).

A Few Green Leaves (London: Macmillan, 1980; New York: E. P. Dutton, 1980).

An Unsuitable Attachment (London: Macmillan, 1982; New York: E. P. Dutton, 1982).

Crampton Hodnet (London: Macmillan, 1985).

An Academic Question (London: Macmillan, 1986).

'Across a Crowded Room', *New Yorker* 55 (16 July 1979) 34–9.

'In Defence of the Novel: Why you Shouldn't Have to Wait until the Afternoon', *The Times*, 22 February 1978, p. 18.

A Very Private Eye: An Autobiography in Diaries and Letters, ed. Hazel Holt and Hilary Pym (London: Macmillan, 1984; New York: E. P. Dutton, 1984).

UNPUBLISHED WORKS BY BARBARA PYM

The papers of Barbara Pym, including manuscripts of published ' and unpublished novels and short stories, literary papers and notebooks, diaries and correspondences, are in the Bodleian Library, Oxford.

STUDIES OF BARBARA PYM

The *Barbara Pym Newsletter*, ed. Mary Anne Schofield (St Bonaventure University) carries a regular survey of Pym Scholarship.

(i) BOOK-LENGTH STUDIES

Benet, Diane, *Something to Love: Barbara Pym's Novels* (Columbia, Missouri: University of Missouri Press 1986).

Long, Robert Emmet, *Barbara Pym* (New York: Ungar, 1986).

Rossen, Janice, *The World of Barbara Pym* (London: Macmillan, 1986).

Nardin, Jane, *Barbara Pym* (Boston, Mass.: Twayne, 1985).

(ii) ARTICLES AND REVIEWS

Ableman, Paul, 'Genteelism' (review of *The Sweet Dove Died*), *Spectator*, 8 July 1978, p. 26.

Ackroyd, Peter, 'Manufacturing Miss Pym' (review of *A Very Private Eye*), *The Times Literary Supplement*, 3 August 1984, p. 861.

——, 'Minor Passions at a Good Address' (review of *The Sweet Dove Died*), *The Times*, 16 July 1978, p. 41.

——, 'Survival of the Faithful' (review of *An Unsuitable Attachment*), *The Times*, 21 February 1982, p. 43.

Auchinglass, Eve, 'Surprises of Comedy and Sadness' (review of *A Few Green Leaves*), *New York Times Book Review*, 1 February 1981, pp. 9, 25.

Bailey, Paul, 'The Art of the Ordinary' (review of *A Few Green Leaves*), *Observer*, 27 October 1980, p. 29.

——, 'A Novelist Rediscovered' (review of *Quartet in Autumn* and *Excellent Women* and *A Glass of Blessings*), *Observer*, 25 September 1977, p. 25.

Boeth, Richard, 'Brief Lives' (review of *Quartet in Autumn*), *Newsweek*, 23 October 1978, pp. 123–5.

Brookner, Anita, 'The Bitter Fruits of Rejection' (review of *Barbara Pym* by Robert Emmet Long), *Spectator*, 19 July 1986, pp. 30–1.

Brothers, Barbara, 'Women Victimized by Fiction: Living and Loving in the Novels by Barbara Pym', in *Twentieth-Century Women Novelists*, ed. Thomas F. Staley (Totowa, NJ: Barnes and Noble, 1982) pp. 61–80.

Broyard, Anatole, 'A Funnier Jane Austen' (review of *No Fond Return of Love*), *New York Times*, 1 January 1983, p. 10.

——, review of *A Very Private Eye*, *New York Times*, 15 June 1984, p. C21.

Burkhardt, Charles, 'An Unpolished Novel by Pym' (review of *An Academic Question*), *Philadelphia Inquirer*, 2 November 1986, p. S6.

——, 'Barbara Pym and the Africans', *Twentieth-Century Literature*, 29 (1983) 45–53.

Butler, Marilyn, 'Keeping up with Jane Austen' (review of *An Unsuitable Attachment*), *London Review of Books*, 6–19 May 1982, pp. 16–17.

Cabisher, Hortense, 'Enclosures: Barbara Pym', *New Criterion*, September 1982, pp. 53–6.

Campbell, James, 'Kitchen Window' (review of *An Unsuitable Attachment*), *New Statesman*, 19 February 1982, p. 25.

Carey, John, 'Pym's Little Ironies' (review of *A Very Private Eye*), *The Times*, 22 July 1984, p. 41.

Cecil, Lord David, 'Barbara Pym', *Journal of the Royal Society of Literature*, Biennial Report 1980–1, pp. 25–6.

Clapp, Susannah, 'Genteel Reminders' (review of *The Sweet Dove Died*), *The Times Literary Supplement*, 7 July 1978, p. 757.

Clemens, Walter, 'An Unnoticed World' (review of *A Glass of Blessings*), *Newsweek*, 14 April 1980, p. 96.

Cunningham, Valentine, 'A World of Ordinary Gentlefolk' (review of *An Unsuitable Attachment*), *Observer*, 21 February 1982, p. 32.

Dick, Kay, 'The Reluctant Spinster' (review of *A Very Private Eye*), *Spectator*, 18 August 1984, p. 23.

Dinnage, Rosemary, 'Comic, Sad, Indefinite' (review of *A Very Private Eye*), *New York Review of Books*, 16 August 1984, pp. 15–16.

Dorris, Michael, review of *Crampton Hodnet*, *New York Times Book Review*, 1 September 1958, p. 12.

Duchene, Anne, 'Handing on Loneliness' (review of *An Unsuitable Attachment*), *The Times Literary Supplement*, 26 February 1982, p. 214.

Feinstein, Elaine, (review of *A Few Green Leaves*), *The Times*, 17 July 1980, p. 11.

Fenton, James, 'The Passionate Spinster who Found Humor' (review of *A Very Private Eye*), *The Times*, 19 July 1984, p. 10.

——, 'A Team of Those Old Oxford Blues' (review of *Crampton Hodnet*. *The Times*, 20 June 1985, p. 11.

Fuller, Edmund, 'Finding a Lifetime Friend in a Writer's Work' (review of *A Glass of Blessings*), *Wall Street Journal*, 20 October 1980, p. 26.

——, 'An Anthropologist of the English Middle Class' (review of *An Unsuitable Attachment*), *Wall Street Journal*, 25 May 1982, p. 30.

——, 'Stylish High Comedy and Astute Perception' (review of *Less than Angels*), *Wall Street Journal*, 2 March 1981, p. 16.

Glendinning, Victoria, 'The Best High Comedy' (review of *Excellent Women* and *Quartet in Autumn*), *New York Times Book Review*, 24 December 1978, p. 8.

Kakutani, Michiko, (review of *Some Tame Gazelle*), *New York Times*, 5 August 1983, p. C22.

Kaufman, Anthony, 'The Short Fiction of Barbara Pym', *Twentieth Century Literature*, Spring 1986, pp. 50–77.

Kemp, Peter, 'Grave Comedy' (review of *A Few Green Leaves*), *Listener*, 17 July 1980, p. 89.

King, Francis, 'Fairly Excellent Women' (review of *A Few Green Leaves*), *Spectator*, 19 July 1980, pp. 21–2.

Larkin, Philip, 'The World of Barbara Pym', *Times Literary Supplement*, 11 March 1977, p. 260.

Lenhart, Maria, 'Quiet Novels Earn Belated Applause' (review of *Quartet in Autumn* and *Excellent Women*), *Christian Science Monitor*, 8 November 1978, p. 18.

Levin, Bernard, 'Middle Marches . . .' (review of *A Few Green Leaves*), *The Times*, 27 July 1980, p. 40.

Liddell, Robert, 'Two Friends: Barbara Pym and Ivy Compton-Burnett', *London Magazine*, August–September 1984, pp. 59–69.

Marsh, Pamela, 'Pym–Subtle and Accomplished' (review of *No Fond Return of Love*), *Christian Science Monitor*, 29 December 1982, p. 15.

Miller, Karl, 'Ladies in Distress' (review of *Excellent Women* and *Quartet in Autumn*), *New York Review of Books*, 9 November, pp. 24–5.

Milton, Edith, 'Worlds in Miniature' (review of *An Unsuitable Attachment*), *New York Times Book Review*, 20 June 1982, p. 11.

'Miss Barbara Pym: Novelist of Distinctive Qualities', *The Times*, 14 January 1980, p. 14.

Moorehead, Caroline, 'How Barbara Pym Was Rediscovered after 16 Years out in the Cold', *The Times*, 14 September 1977, p. 11.

'Notable' (review of *Quartet in Autumn*), *Time*, 9 October 1978, pp. 114–15.

Paulin, Tom, 'Books and Writers' (review of *Quartet in Autumn*), *Encounter*, January 1978, p. 72.

Pippett, Aileen, 'Observers Observed' (review of *Less than Angels*), *New York Times Book Review*, 31 March 1957, p. 33.

'Reputations Revisited', *The Times Literary Supplement*, 21 January 1977, pp. 66–8. (Includes Larkin's and Lord David Cecil's claims for Pym as an underrated writer.)

Rowse, A. L., 'Austen Mini?' (review of *Excellent Women* and *A Glass of Blessings*), *Punch*, 19 October 1977, pp. 732–4.

Rubin, Merle, (review of *A Very Private Eye*), *Christian Science Monitor*, 23 August 1984, p. 21.

Seymour, Miranda, 'Spinsters in their Prime' (review of *Crampton Hodnet*), *The Times Literary Supplement*, 28 June 1985, p. 720.

Shrimpton, Nicholas, 'Bucolic Bones' (review of *A Few Green Leaves*), *New Statesman*, 15 August 1980, p. 17.

Smith, Robert, 'How Pleasant to Know Miss Pym', *Ariel*, 2 (1971) 63–8.

Strouse, Jean, 'Tempest in a Teacup' (review of *No Fond Return of Love*), *Newsweek*, 24 January 1983, pp. 68–9.

Thwaite, Anthony, 'Delicate Manoeuvres' (review of *The Sweet Dove Died*), *Observer*, 9 July 1978, p. 25.

Toomey, Philippa, (review of *Quartet in Autumn, Excellent Women,* and *A Glass of Blessings*), *The Times*, 15 September 1977, p. 18.

Treglown, Jeremy, 'Snob Story' (review of *The Sweet Dove Died*), *New Statesman*, 7 July 1978, p. 27.

'Trouble Brewing' (review of *Less than Angels*), *The Times Literary Supplement*, 18 November 1955, p. 685.

Updike, John, 'Lem and Pym' (review of *Excellent Women*), *New Yorker*, 26 February 1979, pp. 115–21.

Wilson, A. N., 'St Barbara-in-the-Precinct' (review of *An Unsuitable Attachment*), *Spectator*, 20 February 1982, pp. 22–3.

——, 'Thinking of Being Them' (review of *A Few Green Leaves*), *The Times Literary Supplement*, 18 July 1980, p. 799.

Wyndham, Francis, 'The Gentle Power of Barbara Pym' (review of *Quartet in Autumn, Excellent Women* and *A Glass of Blessings*), *The Times*, 18 September 1977, p. 41.

Index